A Study in Forgery

Also from Westphalia Press
westphaliapress.org

The Idea of the Digital University

France and New England
Volumes 1, 2, & 3

Treasures of London

The History of Photography

L'Enfant and the Freemasons

Baronial Bedrooms

Making Trouble for Muslims

Material History and
Ritual Objects

Paddle Your Own Canoe

Opportunity and Horatio Alger

Careers in the Face of Challenge

Bookplates of the Kings

Collecting American Presidential
Autographs

Freemasonry in Old Buffalo

Callinicus

Social Satire and the
Modern Novel

The Essence of Harvard

Ivanhoe Masonic Quartettes

A Definitive Commentary
on Bookplates

James Martineau and
Rebuilding Theology

No Bird Lacks Feathers

Gilded Play

Earthworms, Horses, and
Living Things

The Man Who Killed
President Garfield

Anti-Masonry and the
Murder of Morgan

Understanding Art

Crime 3.0

Fishing the Florida Keys

Collecting Old Books

Masonic Secret Signs and
Passwords

The Thomas Starr King Dispute

Earl Warren's Masonic Lodge

Dante and His Time

Mr. Garfield of Ohio

The Wisdom of Thomas
Starr King

The French Foreign Legion

War in Syria

Naturism Comes to the
United States

New Sources on Women and
Freemasonry

Designing, Adapting, Strategizing
in Online Education

Gunboat and Gun-runner

Meeting Minutes of Naval Lodge
No. 4 F.A.A.M

A Study in Forgery

by Scaevola

with a new introduction by
Katherine Mead-Brewer

WESTPHALIA PRESS
An imprint of Policy Studies Organization

A Study in Forgery
All Rights Reserved © 2014 by Policy Studies Organization

Westphalia Press
An imprint of Policy Studies Organization
1527 New Hampshire Ave., NW
Washington, D.C. 20036
dgutierrezs@ipsonet.org

ISBN-13: 978-1935907497
ISBN-10: 1935907492

Updated material and comments on this edition
can be found at the Westphalia Press website:
www.westphaliapress.org

Introduction
to the New Edition

A Study in Forgery is a peculiar read focused upon Poland's struggle for freedom and independence from Soviet Russia in the first quarter of the 20th century. Written under a pseudonym in the height of World War II (published in London by 1945), this book is not only a valuable read for the arguments it contains but for the historical treasure its writing style possesses. But perhaps the most appropriate place to begin an introduction to this book is in an examination of its title: A Study in Forgery. One might assume from such a moniker that the work centers on some act of forging documents or monies, when in fact the forgery they describe throughout the text has little to do with the simple act of an illegally copied document: this is a study of the forgeries of peace and cultural acceptance. This is a study of the forgery Soviet Russia attempted to perpetrate upon the rest of the world through the cultural domination of Poland in order to paint a portrait of Polish desire for communism and Soviet rule.

As Scaevola explains,

> History has not known yet a forgery on such a scale,...[as this] sham prepared with so much premeditation and forethought by a tiny minority supported by a foreign power and its secret police.

In other words, this is not another textbook aimed at illuminating some new theory-heavy angle on the minutest details of World War II but a bold and clear outcry against a great injustice. Moreover, as you might be able to tell from just that snippet of Scaevola's original introduction, this is a study that doesn't read like your typical history textbook either. Rather, this study reads more as a persuasive, enraged demand for Allied forces to recognize the wool the Soviets are attempting to pull over their eyes – a plea for the Allied forces to see that the Polish people desire freedom and the reestablishment of their own government. In this way, the work reads more like a desperate letter to a friend than a strictly historical account or political argument.

But before launching into the emotion and whirlwind of the text itself, it is first necessary to take a few steps back and give a bit more contextualization to this study in forgery.

Though Poland currently operates under a constitution from the late 1990s, its roots extend as far back as the 10th century. And, while Poland's 20th century dealings with Germany and Russia play most commonly in our modern imagination, Poland has been battling Germany, Russia, and its other neighbors since the very beginning. But let's fast-forward to Poland's golden age in the 16th century. During this time, Poland allied with Lithuania and "maintained an empire that reached from the Baltic to the Black Sea" – an alliance that would eventually culminate into "a unified Polish-Lithuanian state...created by the Union of Lublin (1596)."[1] Yet, despite this already significant kingdom, during much of this period, Poland "was occupied by attempts to conquer Russia."[2]

During the 17th century, Poland was actually "much more influential and powerful than Russia" (with Poland's armies even invading Moscow in 1611); in fact, it wasn't until the latter half of the century that things began to shift back into Russia's favor.[3] In the 1700s, after nearly a full century of almost constant war,

---

1 "Poland," *Columbia Electronic Encyclopedia, 6th Ed.* New York: Columbia University Press, 2013. 1-6p. Web. EBSCO*host*. September 2013.
2 Ibid.
3 Ozbay, Fatih, and Bulent Aras, "Polish-Russian Relations: History, Geography, and Geopolitics," *East European Quarterly, 1.XLII (2008):* 28.

Russia made a bold move on Poland by ensuring that Stanislaus II was crowned king of Poland (thanks especially to the work of Russia's Catherine II and Prussia's Frederick II).[4] After this Russian advance on the Polish throne, the Russian military beat back any and all Polish opposition and protestation until, after a series of partition negotiations between Prussia and Russia, Poland effectively disappeared by 1795, with the "largest share" of the former nation going to Russia.[5] Many Poles fled what remained of their country, seeking refuge in France and the Ottoman Empire with only "this negative Russian involvement" to use "as a glue to preserve their national identity" – a national identity that would go without a nation for the next 123 years.[6] And it is precisely this history of almost constant back-and-forth warring and conquering between these two nations that is often neglected in commentary on Polish-Russian relations today. As Fatih Ozbay and Bulent Aras recognize in "Polish-Russian Relations: History, Geography, and Geopolitics,"

> There is a tendency to explain the Russian-Polish relations through the impact of a number of recent and short term developments. However, the roots of the problematic situation should be found in more than a thousand years of historical relations.[7]

But the story, as Scaevola will soon demonstrate (though they skip a century or so ahead), hardly ends here.

After a nearly 150-year series of continuous gains and losses, brave revolts and crushing defeats, the Polish people finally regained some semblance of independence when they fought back against the Russians in World War I.[8] By 1919, not only had Poland proclaimed its independence and regained access to the

4 "Poland," *Columbia Electronic Encyclopedia, 6th Ed.* New York: Columbia University Press, 2013. 1-6p. Web. EBSCO*host*. September 2013.
5 Ibid.
6 Ozbay, Fatih, and Bulent Aras, "Polish-Russian Relations: History, Geography, and Geopolitics," *East European Quarterly, 1.XLII (2008):* 29.
7 Ibid., 27.
8 "Poland," *Columbia Electronic Encyclopedia, 6th Ed.* New York: Columbia University Press, 2013. 1-6p. Web. EBSCO*host*. September 2013.

Baltic Sea, but it had also had Prussian Poland forcibly returned to it from Germany thanks to the Treaty of Versailles.[9] After this, one can easily imagine the beaten Russia maintaining a wounded, even jealous eye upon Poland – feelings dangerously inflamed in 1939 when Poland refused "to allow Soviet troops to march across Poland in case of conflict with Germany."[10] Poland's unwillingness to work with these attempted Allied negotiations with the Soviets (combined with Soviet fears of another confrontation with Germany), ultimately resulted in the Soviets partnering with Germany over a Non-Aggression Treaty and, eventually, over a partition agreement known as the Molotov-Ribbentrop Pact,[11] agreeing to give Germany power over Western Poland and Soviet Russia power of Eastern Poland.[12] Then, within a month of this Non-Aggression Treaty, Poland found itself invaded once more by both Germany and Russia, an invasion that launched the horrors of World War II – an invasion that spurred Scaevola to pen this impassioned plea for freedom.

Against this backdrop of almost constant war with Russia, Scaevola writes out against not simply the attempted conquest, but against the methods by which Russia attempted it. As Scaevola explains, "In the good old times of yore when life was simpler though not so civilized, conquests were effected with the utmost straightforwardness," but today,

> The conquerors have decided, in a tacit world-wide understanding, that conquest should henceforth be effected from within, and that the utmost care should be taken to gather proof that it was in full accordance with the desires and wishes of the conquered.

---

9 Ibid.

10 Ibid.

11 Ozbay, Fatih, and Bulent Aras, "Polish-Russian Relations: History, Geography, and Geopolitics," *East European Quarterly, 1.XLII (2008):* 30.

12 "Poland," *Columbia Electronic Encyclopedia, 6th Ed.* New York: Columbia University Press, 2013. 1-6p. Web. EBSCO*host*. September 2013.

Thus, though wars were once fought with great slaughter, lands claimed, maps changed, and that be that, wars in Scaevola's world are no longer launched for the desire for land alone – they are wars of cultural conquest. In fact, through the fire of sharp, biting rhetoric, Scaevola is prompted to suggest that even the Nazis were preferable conquerors to the Soviets as the Nazis, "with [their] acts of unbelievable cruelty and [their] crazy passion for annihilation, [were] at least understandable…. He came to destroy and did not make any pretense of friendship." So though the Nazis sought to destroy Poland, at least they, unlike the Soviets, showed no desire to try to convince the rest of the world that the Polish people were happy about being so viciously conquered.

Throughout the book, Scaevola's seething over this forgery is startlingly obvious, evidenced by chapter titles such as "'Free Election' Or 'Swindle Democracy?'" and brazen language such as: "Mundus vult decipi (the world is easily deceived), provided it is given something to sweeten the deceit. The Nazis failed to do that. The Soviets, in accordance with their lip-service to political democracy, had not." Through this passion, Scaevola presents the Soviet Russian attempt at conquering Poland as the work of an evil mastermind bent on consuming every shred of what was once Poland and Polish. One can only surmise from this impassioned style (combined with the author(s)'s desire to remain anonymous) that the author(s) is most probably Polish and writing from within the fray. After all, it only makes sense that the author(s) would choose to remain anonymous if they viewed their anonymity as a necessary precaution to protect themselves and their families from Soviet backlash. During the 1940s, Poland wasn't a safe place for even those writers who converted to the communist cause, let alone those who stood up against it. Consider, for example, Polish poet Aleksander Wat, who served for a time as the "editor of the Marxist Literary Monthly" yet who still was unable to flee eastward as the Nazis invaded from the west thanks to Soviet secret police that arrested and exiled him as well as his family to Kazakhstan.[13]

13 Caldwell, Christopher, "When Evil Was a Social System: The moral burdens of living under communist rule in Eastern Europe," *The New Republic*, 13 July 2013. Web. 17 Sept. 2013. http://www.newrepublic. com/article/113574/when-evil-was-social-system-moral-burdens-communist-rule.

When Wat swallowed a bottle of sleeping pills in 1967, his suicide note simply read: "Do not save me," such was the guilt he experienced for "the part he had played as perpetrator – as one who had made the intellectual world safe for Stalinism."[14] In his autobiography, Wat wrote: "the loss of freedom, tyranny, abuse, hunger would all have been easier to bear if not for the compulsion to call them freedom, justice, the good of the people…."[15] But this was how, according to Scaevola, the Soviets managed to so deftly sweep Poland's feet out from under it: by poisoning Poland at every level from its writers to its armies; by dragging "the names of national heroes…out of the arsenal of history" to misapply them elsewhere; by infiltrating and exploiting groups like the Polish Women's League and the Polish Boy Scouts;[16] and by appropriating "the names and the tradition of the [Polish political] parties" until no one, not even many Polish, could see clearly quite how the crime had been committed. As Anne Applebaum so succinctly puts it,

> Before a nation can be rebuilt, its citizens need to understand how it was destroyed in the first place: how its institutions were undermined, how its language was twisted, how its people were manipulated.[17]

But the real question for this work becomes, what meaning does it hold for us today? What can this snapshot of Polish outrage against Soviet Russia tell us about ourselves in the here-and-now?

The keenest part of this story is Scaevola's recognition of the shift from geographic to cultural conquests in modern warfare and it is in this that we may begin to understand the broader range of this text. Of course, whereas Russia's systematic work in the 1940s to infiltrate and transform every level of Poland's political, economic, and social spheres was considered an act

---

14 Ibid.
15 Wat quoted in, Ibid.
16 Ibid.
17 Applebaum, Anne, *Iron Curtain: The Crushing of Eastern Europe, 1945-1956*. New York: Doubleday, 2012. 470.

of war, today such acts often flourish under the guise of less sensational monikers, such as capitalism.

In academia, we often throw around terms like "cultural appropriation" and "cultural assimilation" – some would argue we now do so to the point of rendering these terms all but meaningless. Even still, these terms are quickly becoming more and more important to some as weapons to protect cultural artifacts and practices while becoming outdated to other minds as relics of a pre-globalized world. However, regardless of one's opinions on concepts of cultural authenticity, appropriation, and assimilation, there is no denying that it is through the vast reach of capitalist powers that we are beginning to see these forces take effect on a global scale, whether for good or ill. And while it is often without malice that capitalist powers affect such cultural changes abroad, the intent here seldom changes the action. Much as Soviet Russia wanted cultural control of Poland in order to cease the centuries-old back-and-forth between them, capitalists seek financial control of foreign markets in order to cease the back-and-forth of international economic competitiveness. Of course, more than simply desiring unquestioned dominance in foreign markets, capitalist powers now also desire to project to the rest of the world a sense of caring for and empowerment of those foreign peoples they seek to financially dominate. A desire eerily similar in scope to Scaevola's allegations against Soviet Russia:

> ...the utmost care should be taken to gather proof that [the conquest] was in full accordance with the desires and wishes of the conquered. The conquest was to be made, as it were, on behalf of the conquered, and in the full-glory of Democracy.

By now, images of U.S. leaders and thinkers like Milton Friedman might be swimming to mind. Of course, it's important to note that Friedman is by no means a Stalin-esque mass murderer, but much of his recent "economic 'shock treatment'" strategy[18] speaks to the

---

18 Klein, Naomi. *The Shock Doctrine: The Rise of Disaster Capitalism.* New York: Picador, 2007. 8.

key issue of Scaevola's brand of forgery: when is a foreign power a truly desirable and beneficial force and when is a foreign power simply working to veil its own greed in superficial shows of benefit toward those they profit from?

As Naomi Klein argues in The Shock Doctrine, Friedman began exercising a version of his "shock treatment" – or, as she puts it, "first learned how to exploit large-scale shock or crisis" – while advising Chilean dictator, General Augusto Pinochet in the 1970s.[19] During this time, Chile was still reeling from Pinochet's coup and a severe wave of hyperinflation; and, in order to take full advantage of this chaotic state, Friedman suggested rapid and intensive capitalist transformation of the Chilean economy including "tax cuts, free trade, privatized services, cuts to social spending and deregulation" – advice that resulted in "the most extreme capitalist makeover ever attempted anywhere."[20] In other words, Friedman oversaw the total upheaval of Chilean culture – following their violent coup and economic disaster, Friedman swept in to prompt Pinochet to go ahead and transform every other possible facet of Chilean life. These actions bloomed into a full and firm U.S. economic philosophy known as the Chicago School movement – a movement that has continued to impose capitalist goals, practices, and agendas on foreign nations for decades since, or, as Klein puts it, that has continued "conquering territory around the world since the seventies…."[21]

Throughout A Study in Forgery, Scaevola provides us with evidence of Soviet Russia's attempt to pass off their conquest of Poland as somehow not only beneficial to the Polish peoples but also as something they desired. However, as Scaevola so succinctly phrases it:

> Poland is one of the many countries which have recently experienced the new technique of conquest. She is one of the many nations that desire real freedom and not the pretense of it.

---

19 Ibid.
20 Ibid.
21 Ibid., 13.

And it is this message and these questions – when is foreign influence and involvement necessary, desired, coercive, or gluttonous? – that we must come away from Scaevola's work still considering. In our increasingly globalized world, forgeries and cultural conquests are becoming easier and easier to perpetrate — the obstacle now lies in not only being able to tell the difference between a forgery and the article genuine, but in knowing how to act upon such knowledge.

Katherine Mead-Brewer

Bibliography

Applebaum, Anne. Iron Curtain: The Crushing of Eastern Europe, 1945-1956. New York: Doubleday, 2012. 470.

Caldwell, Christopher. "When Evil Was a Social System: The moral burdens of living under communist rule in Eastern Europe." The New Republic. 13 July 2013. Web. 17 Sept. 2013. http://www.newrepublic.com/article/113574/when-evil-was-social-system-moral-burdens-communist-rule.

Klein, Naomi. The Shock Doctrine: The Rise of Disaster Capitalism. New York: Picador, 2007.

Ozbay, Fatih, and Bulent Aras. "Polish-Russian Relations: History, Geography, and Geopolitics." East European Quarterly, 1.XLII (2008): 27-42.

"Poland." Columbia Electronic Encyclopedia, 6th Ed. New York: Columbia University Press, 2013. 1-6p. Web. EBSCOhost. September 2013.

A Study in Forgery

By
SCAEVOLA

CONTENTS

INTRODUCTION

In the good old times of yore when life was simpler though not so civilised, conquests were effected with the utmost straightforwardness. After the usual slaughter, the victor did not ask the conquered what rulers they would like to have, or under what political system they would feel most efficient and happy. He simply incorporated the vanquished nation into his realm and appointed a lieutenant to rule it as his pleasure dictated.

Impartiality compels us to acknowledge that there was a certain charm about conquest in the days of yore. There was no hypocritical concealment of the true character of the operation, and the victor was not a busybody who would take pains to show that his deed was in accordance with the will of his newly acquired people. Not only that. Not infrequently he even contented himself with formal incorporation, and, provided his lieutenant was not a tyrant by nature, they both let the conquered people or tribe continue to live more or less as they wished, retaining their gods, their set of beliefs and their specific brand of culture. In such cases, not only was the conquest itself more straightforward than nowadays but sometimes the results thereof had a more superficial character.

The modern civilised world has repudiated war and conquest. Our delicate comprehension of other peoples' rights, our attachment to our own freedom and respect for the individual character of every man and every nation, cannot but shudder at the mere thought of conquest and war. The rulers have followed suit in their own peculiar way.

More refined methods of conquest have been invented so as to avoid direct clashes with all the fine feelings engendered by the progress of culture and civilisation. At the same time, the consequences of the conquest have been made to reach deeper into the life of the conquered.

The conquerors have decided, in a tacit world-wide understanding, that conquest should henceforth be effected from within, and that the utmost care should be taken to gather proof that it was in full accordance with the desires and wishes of the conquered. The conquest was to be made, as it were, on behalf of the conquered, and in the full-glory of Democracy. The appearances of national independence were to be preserved. However, the conquered state's political, economic and social system was to undergo deep and radical changes, ruthlessly eliminating all elements unable to adapt themselves to the new structure.

The modern technique of conquest was applied for the first time when two new republics, Tuva and Outer Mongolia, were carved out of Chinese territory on the border of the U.S.S.R.

Visitors to the Metropole Hotel in Moscow can admire delegations in Mongolian dress and in Soviet officers' uniforms, arriving from time to time in the capital of the Soviet Empire, after a long journey from their native lands. In accordance with their Oriental customs they bring gifts for Soviet dignitaries, and thoroughly enjoy the opportunity of visiting what in their opinion is the most modern capital of the world. After a few weeks' stay in Moscow, they leave for home. In the meantime, new gifts are collected, and a new delegation prepares for the same journey.

The chief duty of these countries consists in supplying certain contingents of recruits of whom more will probably be heard when the European chapter of the present war comes to a close, and when the Asiatic chapter unfolds itself in full. Needless to add, both Mongol republics are " people's republics," independent and free.

The story of the conquest of Manchuria by Japan and of the subsequent formation of an " independent " Manchukuo is also very illuminating.

It began in September, 1931, when the Japanese availed themselves of an " incident " whose true origin has never been satisfactorily established. After protracted fighting, which, in view of the vast areas involved, took many months, the Japanese found puppets willing to pose as representatives of the Manchu people, and soon had the impudence to assert before the League of Nations that the annexation of Manchu territory was a measure of self-defence, and that the new State of Manchuko had been founded by the spontaneous will of the people (cf., Japanese note of February 27th, 1933). This " spontaneous will " has been best described in the Lytton Report, according to which the Japanese " made use of the names and actions of certain Chinese individuals, and took advantage of certain minorities among the inhabitants, who had grievances against the former (i.e., Chinese, not ours) Administration.

At first the world did not grasp the import of this new method of conquest. Only when it was applied in the very heart of the civilised world was it understood. Adolf Hitler improved upon it, although, as applied by him, it did not yet attain the acme of perfection. A Fifth Column was created, recruited mostly from German minorities, with the task of undermining States from within. It was proved that, in order to effect a conquest, it was not indispensable to use military force or to organise a revolution. By the mere threat of force, Hitler was able to seize Austria, Czecho-slovakia and the Memel area. Direct incorporation, division, preservation of a shadow independence under a Protector's rule, or even, as in the case of Slovakia, fictitious independ-ence, were the procedures adopted. All these conquests—as Hitler himself boasted—were effected without bloodshed. We may add that from the strictly formal point of view they were effected according to the letter of the law and in virtue of the alleged consent of the nations concerned and their parliaments.

The method was further perfected when the three Baltic republics, Estonia, Latvia and Lithuania, were conquered. Communist parties representing less than 1 per cent. of the people here assumed the role of the Fifth Column. In that capacity these parties are superior to the German minorities in Hitler's employ, since people of all nationalities, races and creeds may join them, and since the dynamite they use is not of such poor quality as that of *Mein Kampf*. The struggle they wage is—so they allege—a struggle for the liberation of the working man. The incorporation of a State into the Soviet Union is only an unforeseen and subsequent by-product of political and social evolution. True, in all cases Russia also had to use military force, but—as it was later demonstrated through plebiscites—enthusiastic meetings and the unanimous resolutions of the parliaments of these countries—it was the " people " itself that had called upon the Red Army divisions to help destroy " native reaction." The conquest thus brought about was full and complete. The countries concerned carried out fundamental changes in their social and political structure and, almost overnight, became enthusiastic admirers of a new unknown system and reorganised their life accordingly.

History went on. One after another the new creatures of Nazi barbarism and perfidy were emerging in the process of the subjugation of Europe. Quisling, Degrelle, Moravec, Laval and many others made their appearance in the forefront of decay. The free world slowly realised what system was being introduced and what it meant. This realisation found its true expression in the Atlantic Charter, this confession of faith of the nations fighting for democracy, justice, equal distribution of wealth, progress and freedom. The first three articles of the Charter contain principles which, if they crystallise into reality, may well render impossible future wars and mutual extermination among the inhabitants of the globe now so essentially one.

It is against this general background that the story that has been told in these pages has to be read and understood. Poland is one of the many countries which have recently experienced the new technique of conquest. She is one of the many nations that desire real freedom and not the pretence of it.

The story told is one of forgery. We hope that it may be useful both as a study in history and in the modern perverted ways of political behaviour.

London, March, 1945.

CHAPTER I

AN UNFINISHED PRELUDE

Few of our readers still remember the war that raged in 1919 and 1920 between Poland and Soviet Russia for the possession of a vast stretch of lands between the Bug and the Dnieper, which up to the Partitions of the XVIII century had been for four hundred years in the possession of Poland, acquired mainly through voluntary union with the ancient Duchy of Lithuania, and which had a strong admixture of Polish population, very marked in the West, less so towards the East.

In the summer of 1920, during the Soviet offensive directed against Warsaw, a group of Polish Communists was organised behind the Russian lines to play the role of a Soviet-sponsored authority in Poland. This group proclaimed itself at Białystok a " Polish Provisional Revolutionary Government."

Feliks Dzierżyński, the famous head of the Soviet Cheka (now NKVD), Feliks Kon, Julian Marchlewski and Alfred Lampe, were its most prominent leaders.

Soon, the would-be rulers of a future Soviet Poland started organising an army of their own, and issued in bad Polish a fiery proclamation to the Polish soldiers. The proclamation ran as follows :

" Polish Soldiers ! . . . The Red Army entering Polish territory is not guided by imperialist greed. It brings the working people of Poland help to fight for liberation from under the yoke of the nobility and the bourgeoisie. It is fully conscious that only a workers' and peasants' Poland can protect Soviet Russia from the greed of Polish and foreign imperialist aggressors. Fighting for its own freedom it also fights for ours. We extend our welcome to the Red Army who is not our enemy but a brother happier than ourselves because he has already been liberated. Our main task at present is to join forces with the Red Army and jointly conquer our common enemy. This is our duty towards the working people of Poland. ·

We call upon you to fulfil this duty ! Form Soldiers' Councils ! Take prisoner your officers and hasten to Warsaw together with the Red Army, so as to save from destruction whatever may yet be saved after the landlords' rule. Every wasted moment threatens thousands of people with death from starvation ! To deeds, comrades ! Fulfil your duty ! Proletarians unite with proletarians against exploiters. Let a Polish Red Army keep pace with the Russian Red Army in the grand struggle for the liberation of the working people !

Be quick, workers and peasants. We call you to a great deed, to the '' final struggle '' against the world of exploitation ! ''

However, soon they were bitterly disappointed. The peasantry, the workers and the working intelligentsia of Poland, showed by their attitude that they did not want social reform on the Communist pattern and internal bloodshed after the Russian fashion. Not only that. Called for the defence of the country by their acknowledged Peasant Party and Socialist leaders, they flocked en masse to the ranks of the Polish Army, to repel the foreign invasion.

In mid-August, 1920, the Red Army was defeated at the outskirts of Warsaw, and repulsed much further east.

On October 12th, 1920, a preliminary treaty of peace was signed between Poland and Soviet Russia-Ukraine, to be replaced on March 18th, 1921, by a final treaty, known as '' the Treaty of Riga.''

We may be excused for quoting here also a similar manifesto issued, in equally bad Polish, to Polish soldiers on September 17th, 1939, by the C.-inC. of the Byelorussian Front, Army Commander Kovalev. The analogy is striking :

'' Soldiers of the Polish Army !

The Polish landlords and bourgeois Government which has dragged you into an adventurers' war, has shamelessly disintegrated. It turned out incapable of governing the country and of organising defence. . . . . The Polish Army has suffered a severe defeat from which it is unable to disentangle itself. Death from starvation and destruction threatens your wives, children, brothers and sisters.

. . . . Do not resist the Red Army of Workers and Peasants. Your resistance will not be of any avail to you, and will expose you to destruction. We are coming not as your conquerors but as your class brethren and liberators from the big landlords' and capitalists' oppression.

The great and invincible Red Army brings the working people brotherhood and a happy life inscribed on its banners.

Soldiers of the Polish Army ! Do not shed blood in vain, in defence of the interests of the landlords and the capitalists, alien to you ! . . . . Give up weapons ! Come over to the Red Army. Your freedom and life are assured.''

A frontier line was then agreed upon after prolonged dis-
cussions, which left with Russia the main Ukrainian and
White Ruthenian (Byelorussian) territories.

A period of peace ensued between the two neighbouring
states. The members of the '' Polish Provisional Revolutionary Government '' returned to Russia, which had already
been their spiritual and actual fatherland for quite a long
time, and were allotted other tasks by the Soviet Government. The most famous amongst them, Feliks Dzierżyński,
as head of the much dreaded Cheka reverted to his job
of tracing and eliminating the enemies of the Soviet State.
He is usually rightly ranked amongst its foremost founders.

Whether they cared for it or not, most of them were never
to see Poland again.

PART I

CHAPTER II

" TWO SWIFT BLOWS "

In a speech delivered on October 31st, 1939, at the Extraordinary Fifth Session of the Supreme Soviet of the U.S.S.R., M. V. Molotov, the Soviet Commissar for Foreign Affairs, then also Chairman of the Council of the People's Commissars, said inter alia :—

> " . . . one swift blow to Poland, first by the German Army and then by the Red Army, and nothing was left of this ugly offspring of the Versailles Treaty. . . ."[*]

Let us note in passing that unmistakable emotion rang out in the words of M. Molotov, and that a feeling of delight was discernible in his phrasing.

This, however, is none of our concern here. All that is of interest to us is that the passage quoted from M. Molotov's speech undoubtedly constituted the point of departure for future Soviet policy towards Poland. In Soviet eyes, Poland had become a " nothing," and a " something " was to be found instead to fill up the political vacuum created by the armies of Poland's two giant neighbours.

Such was the Soviet attitude. The less picturesque language of the Soviet note to the Polish Ambassador in Moscow dated September 17th, 1939, summed it up in a more formal manner, alleging that " the Polish State and its Government have, in fact, ceased to exist."[†]

---

[*] Cf. p. 27, Soviet Peace Policy, Four Speeches by V. Molotov, with a Foreword by D. N. Pritt, K.C., M.P., and Biographical Sketch by W. P. and Zelda K. Coates, published for the Anglo-Russian News Bulletin by Lawrence and Wishart Ltd., London, first published 1941, pp. 101.

[†] Cf. p. 189, Republic of Poland, Ministry for Foreign Affairs, Official Documents concerning Polish-German and Polish-Soviet Relations, 1933-1939. The Polish White Book published by authority of the Polish Government by Roy Publishers, New York, pp. 222.

However, no justification could be found for this view in the realities of the situation. On September 17th, when the Red Army entered Poland and when the Soviet note was handed, the Polish armies were still fighting. The official Nazi army gazette, published by the German High Command (*Heeres-Verordnungsblatt, herausgegeben vom Oberkommando des Heeres*), issue of January 2nd, 1940, mentioned as the last battle with the Polish Army on Polish territory the battle of Kock-Adamów (Central Poland) of October 2nd-7th, 1939, and laid down that those who took part in the Polish Campaign should receive the following entry in their military record books : " Campaign against Poland, September 1st, 1939, till October 7th, 1939." On the Soviet side, an operational communiqué was issued by the General Headquarters of the Red Army as late as September 28th, 1939, in which the liquidation of a number of Polish Army units, including five cavalry regiments was announced.

On September 17th, the Polish Government was still functioning on Polish soil controlling an area of about 77,000 square miles, i.e., slightly over half the total area of Poland, inhabited permanently by 13,000,000 people to which were added many big army units and numerous refugees from the territory overrun by the Nazis. Following the Soviet attack of September 17th, the then Government of Poland crossed the frontier into Rumania. Later on, after the resignation of President Moscicki, and in accordance with the Polish Constitution, President Raczkiewicz took office on September 30th, 1939, in Paris, and a new Government headed by the late General Sikorski was sworn in. This government, later presided over by M. Mikolajczyk and now, since November 29th, 1944, by M. Arciszewski, has been recognised by all Allied and neutral Powers, and, in the period July 30th, 1941 —April 25th, 1943, by the U.S.S.R. Since its formation, this Government has taken an active part in the joint war against Germany.

Thus, the Polish State had never ceased legally to exist, nor was there any ground for alleging that " nothing " had been left of Poland after the two " swift blows " of the fateful autumn of 1939.

The Soviet leaders themselves were only too well aware of the purely rhetorical character of their allegations. They were too realistic to lull themselves into a false belief that Nazi-Soviet friendship, as a result of which the two partners had each taken possession of half of Poland, would be of long duration. Sooner or later, war was bound to break out between the two states, and amongst many other problems that of Poland was bound to arise again.

" There can be no question of restoring old Poland," said M. Molotov, further in the speech quoted (ib. p. 29). The solution best adapted to the interests of the Soviet State and of World Communism had therefore to be worked out and prepared in advance, so as not to let events develop in undesirable directions.

In the meantime the problem of the occupied Eastern Poland awaited immediate settlement.

Chapter III

THE FOURTH PARTITION OF POLAND

Ranking in the period of 1386-1696 amongst the foremost powers of Europe, the ancient Polish Republic had since entered upon a path of gradual decline in political and military importance. The eighteenth century saw the quick and decisive rise of her two neighbours, Prussia and Russia. Using force, the two States effected three partitions of the Republic (1772, 1793 and 1795), the last of which brought the Republic's existence to an end. A continuation of the old Commonwealth, the modern Republic of Poland only arose in 1918, towards the end of the First World War.

September, 1939, brought about a fourth partition of Poland, by Nazi Germany, the heir of the Kingdom of Prussia, and by the U.S.S.R., the inheritor of the territories and policies of the former Tsarist Empire.

The partition treaty was concluded on September 28th, 1939, while Polish regular forces were still striving to stem the two tides, and when Poland's capital had not yet been captured by the enemy.* In virtue of the Treaty, which constituted a flagrant breach of international law, Nazi Germany took 72,866 sq. miles or 48.4 per cent. of Polish territory, whilst the Soviet Union was assigned the remaining 77,620 sq. miles or 51.6 per cent. The partition line ran along the rivers Pissa, Bug and San.

On the Bug sector it was identical with a line suggested on July 11th, 1920, by the Allied Powers as provisional demarcaion pending a final settlement of relations between Poland and Soviet Russia, called the " Curzon Line." This partial identity gave rise to frequent misunderstandings in the world press which recently began to revive the forgotten term " Curzon Line " to denote what, in actual fact, ought to be called after its two creators, Molotov and Ribbentrop.

As *Pravda* of September 30th, 1939, asserted in an article written on the occasion of the conclusion of the Partition Treaty, the Ribbentrop-Molotov line was to be final.

> " The boundary line between the State interests of the U.S.S.R. and Germany respectively in the territory of the former Polish State has been accurately and finally fixed. . . . The U.S.S.R. and Germany have come to a final understanding concerning the frontier, peace and order, in the territory where the interests of the two States meet."

---

* Cf. the last communiqué issued by the Warsaw Defence Command on September 29th, as quoted in the Polish White Book, p. 140.

CHAPTER IV

GIFT OF VILNO

Germany divided her spoils into two parts about equal in size. The western part, comprising Pomorze, the Poznań (Posen) area, Silesia, and adjacent stretches of Central Poland, 35,714 sq. miles altogether, was incorporated into the Reich by a decree of the Fuehrer and Chancellor of the Reich, dated October 8th, 1939. The remaining regions of Central Poland, with Warsaw and Cracow, were constituted into what was to be known henceforth as '' the Government General,'' an area of 36,862 sq. miles, subordinated to the Reich and ruled for its exclusive benefit by a Nazi Governor-General directly responsible to Hitler himself (decree of October 12th, 1939).

The procedure applied by the Nazis was simple and crude. They did not bother to pretend that the direct and the indirect annexation of their part of Poland was a result of the wishes of the population. The Soviet procedure was much subtler.

The first sign of Soviet shrewdness was the treaty enforced by the U.S.S.R. on Lithuania on October 10th, 1939*, by which a Polish area of 3,219 sq. miles, adjacent to Lithuanian territory and including the ancient city of Vilno was transferred to the then still independent Baltic Republic. In exchange, Lithuania had to grant the U.S.S.R. the right to set up certain military and air bases on Lithuanian territory.

This transfer of territory may rightly be likened to the killing of several birds with one stone. First, the pro-Nazi Lithuanian nationalist elements were appeased thereby, for some time at least (in June, 1941, they organised a rising against the retreating Red Army). Further, the Polish-

*S. Lozoraitis, a former Lithuanian Minister of Foreign Affairs (1934-38) and Minister in Rome (1938-40), said in a press statement of May, 1941, that '' the Muscovite Government, threatening war, forced Lithuania to sign an agreement on the setting up of Soviet bases in our country,'' the Lithuanian weekly *Iseiviu Draugas* ('' The Emigrés' Friend ''), Bellshill, Scotland, issue of July 4th, 1941.

Lithuanian dispute over Vilno was again inflamed. Last but not least, the gift of Vilno could be presented to liberal world opinion as proof of Soviet magnanimity, and fully justified the Soviet Foreign Commissar's statement to the effect that '' it had been pointed out in the foreign press that there had never been a case in world history of a big country handing over, of its own free will, such a big city to a small State '' (cf. p. 37, Soviet Peace Policy).

Only those with first-hand knowledge of the actual state of affairs knew how much truth there was in the rather inadvertent admission by Molotov that '' the majority of the inhabitants of Vilno are not Lithuanian '' (*ibidem*) and that the Lithuanian minority of Vilno was slightly less than 1 per cent., whereas in the whole of the transferred territory it did not exceed 11.3 per cent.

As later events proved, Vilno was not one of the losses that are never retrieved. A little over eight months later, on June 15th, 1940, the city and the province were back in Soviet hands again, this time with the handsome addition of the whole of Lithuania itself, proclaimed a Soviet Republic.

The gift of Vilno was, however, a marginal issue in view of the small size of the area involved (3,219 sq. miles as against the 77,620 sq. miles of the whole of Eastern Poland).

Of main interest is the treatment reserved to the bulk of the Soviet-conquered territory and this we shall now present to the reader.

CHAPTER V

POLITICAL PURGE

After the entry of the Red Army into Eastern Poland a clean sweep was made of almost everything that was considered undesirable from the Soviet point of view.

The administration of towns and villages was taken over by the Soviet authorities. Members of the autonomous administrative bodies were arrested and imprisoned. A similar fate befell them ajority of higher and lower civil servants.

Equally, all social organisations of any kind, Polish, Ukrainian, Jewish and White Ruthenian (Byelorussian) were dissolved and their property taken over by the Soviets.

Political parties were also affected.

Grown up under a single party régime, some of the Soviet officials sent up for the task could not even understand that there could have been in Poland more than one party.

The worst hit were the three Marxist-Socialist parties of Poland: the Polish Socialist Party, the General Jewish Workers' Union (the Bund) and the Ukrainian Social Democratic Party.

The purge had a twofold purpose. First, it was considered necessary to liquidate for good all the politically active non-Communist elements, especially those with influence on the masses. Then, a clean sweep was to be made before the elections with a view to making the people understand that it was in their own interest to obey the new régime unconditionally and give up any foolish idea of even passive resistance.

Here is a very incomplete list of the leaders of the *Polish Socialist Party* arrested and deported by the Soviet authorities to the U.S.S.R. mostly during the pre-election period :

Stanisław Grylowski—a former Seym* deputy, secretary-general of the Railwaymen's Trade Union, a member of the National Committee of the P.S.P. ; died in prison.

Artur Hausner—a former Seym deputy, a member of the National Committee of the P.S.P. ; died in prison.

Tomasz Kapitułka—leader of the Trade Unions at Bialystok, a member of the National Committee of the P.S.P. ; died in prison.

Jan Szałaśny—leader of the Railwaymen's Trade Union at Stanisławów, a member of the National Committee of the P.S.P. ; died in prison

---

* Seym—the lower chamber of the Polish Parliament, corresponding to the House of Commons in Britain.

Wróbel—a member of the Regional Committee of Trade Unions at Lvov ; died in prison.

Franciszek Przewlocki—chairman of the Regional Committee of the Miners' Federation ; died in prison.

Moroń—deputy-secretary of the Regional Committee of the Miners' Federation at Borysław ; died in prison.

Stanisław Talarek—chairman of the Regional Committee of the Railwaymen's Trade Union at Lvov ; died after being released from prison as a result of the Polish-Soviet Agreement of July 30th, 1941.

Mieczysław Mastek—a former Seym deputy, chairman of the Executive Committee of Railwaymen's Trade Union ; died in London, his health having been ruined in prison.

Zygmunt Piotrowski—a former Seym deputy, secretary-general of the Association of Workers' Universities, a member of the National Committee of the P.S.P. ; fate unknown.*

Wojciech Ożga—former Mayor of Stryj, chairman of the Regional Executive Committee of the P.S.P. at Stryj ; fate unknown.

Aleksander Princ, leader of Socialist youth at Lvov ; fate unknown.†

Dręgiewicz—a lawyer, an active Socialist from Lvov ; died in prison.

Franciszek Hoffmann—chairman of the Association of Communal Workers at Lvov ; fate unknown.

Zygmunt Nowakowski—chairman of the Council of the Workers' Trade Unions at Lvov ; fate unknown.

---

* The note '' fate unknown,'' means that it has not been possible to state where and when the person in question died, though it seems more than probable that he died either during the deportation, in prison or in compulsory labour camp. If no mention has been made, this must be taken to mean that the person in question has been released under the Soviet-Polish Agreement of 1941, and that he is outside the U.S.S.R.

† All the names hitherto mentioned were given in an address by C. Huysmans, Chairman of the Second International, delivered at the Caxton Hall, London, on March 8th, 1943.

Tadeusz Drobut—vice-chairman of the Association of Communal Workers at Lvov ; fate unknown.

Bronisław Skalak—chairman of the Lvov Region of the P.S.P. ; now deputy-chairman of the Polish National Council in London.

Jan Szczyrek—editor-in-chief of the Socialist daily " Dziennik Ludowy " at Lvov ; now a member of the Polish National Council in London.

Jan Kwapiński—chairman of the Executive Committee of Trades Unions ; now Minister in London.

Franciszek Haluch—secretary of the Miners' Federation.

Kazimierz Jaroszewski—then about 65 years old ; secretary of the Association for Building Workers' Houses at Borysław ; chairman of the Trade Union of Non-Manual Workers of the Oil Industry, at Borysław, and chairman of the Chief Council of Workers' Consumer Co-operatives.

Artur Szewczyk—chairman of the Łódź region of the P.S.P.

Witold Czyż—a former vice-mayor of Vilno.

Dr. Jonas—an active Socialist from Lvov.

Kazimierz Petrusewicz—arrested a few days after the entry of the Red Army to Vilno in September, 1939 ; Petrusewicz, born in 1877 at Minsk, was one of the eight founders of the Russian Workers' Socialist Party, to which Lenin and Stalin later acceded. In independent Poland Petrusewicz took part in several Communist trials as counsel for defence ; his fate is not known.

Stanisław Bagiński—leader of the P.S.P. at Vilno ; died or shot in prison.

Michael Ładowski—a Socialist leader from Vilno ; died or shot in prison.

Here is information concerning some leaders of the " Bund " :

Anna Rozenthal—over 60 years of age ; a member of the Central Committee of the Bund ; spent ten years in Tsarist prison ; arrested in Vilno with all members of the local Bund Committee ; shot (without trial) during the evacuation of prisoners in the summer of 1941.

David Batist—a member of the Chief Council of the Bund ; died from exhaustion immediately after release from compulsory labour camp.

Dr. Henryk Szreiber—about 70 ; leader of the Bund at Cracow ; died from exhaustion immediately after release from compulsory labour camp.

A similar fate befell the leaders of *Ukrainian.*workers and peasants :

Ivan Kushnir—secretary of the Regional Committee of Trades Unions at Lvov ; died in prison.

Ivan Kvasnytsia—a former Seym deputy, secretary-general of the Ukrainian Social Democrat Party ; died in prison.

Dr. Volodimir Starosolsky—a member of the Senate ; leader of the Ukrainian Social Democrats at Lvov ; fate unknown.

Dr. Rudolf Skibinsky—a leader of the Ukrainian Social Democrat Party at Lvov ; fate unknown.

Dr. Roman Dombchevsky—leader of the Party at Stryj ; fate unknown.

Osyp Kohut—a member of the Senate ; a Social Radical Leader ; died after release from imprisonment.

Wiktor Alter—a member of the Executive Committee of the International of Trade Unions ; executed.*

Henryk Erlich—a member of the Executive Committee of the Second International ; executed.*

---

* Cf. the speech by Huysmans, and a pamphlet " The Case of Henryk Erlich and Wiktcr Alter," Foreword by Camille Huysmans, publi hed by Liberty Publications . . . for the General Jewish Workers' Union " Bund " of Poland, London, 1943.

This is what the former Soviet Ambassador in Washington wrote in this connection to the President of the American Federation of Labour in a letter dated February 23rd, 1943 :

" I am instructed by Mr. Molotov to inform you of the following facts :

For active subversive work against the Soviet Union and assistance to Polish intelligence organs in armed activities, Erlich and Alter were sentenced to capital punishment in August, 1941.

At the request of the Polish Government, Erlich and Alter were released in September, 1941.

However, after they were set free at the time of the most desperate battles of the Soviet troops against the advancing Hitler army, they resumed their hostile activities, including appeals to the Soviet troops to stop bloodshed and immediately to conclude peace with Germany.

For this they were re-arrested and, in December, 1942, sentenced once more to capital punishment by the Military Collegium of the Supreme Court. This sentence has been carried out in regard to both of them.

Yours sincerely,

Ambassador Maxim Litvinov."

This is what C. Huysmans said about the alleged reasons of this execution :

" Still more disquieting is the fact that they (i.e., the Communists) have not the courage to admit their deeds. . . . They do not justify their actions on the grounds of the differences of opinion which were the real cause. No. They invent insults and slander. Let us examine the case of our friends, Erlich and Alter. Can anyone be found in this hall who would believe for a moment that they, democrats of a high moral level, who for many years had showed so much courage in the front ranks of our struggle—could have committed so mean an act and—let me say—so stupidly infamous, as common treachery ? Erlich and Alter are alleged to be Hitler's agents against Russia, agents of Hitler, who is a sadistic persecutor of their nation and of its friends, and the butcher of the country whose loyal citizens they were.

" No one will believe that—not even in Russia.

" No one."

The leaders of the Right Wing parties were also arrested and deported. A few leaders of the *National Democratic Party* may be mentioned :

Stanisław Głąbiński—a professor at Lvov University ; chairman of the Party at Lvov ; died in imprisonment.

Roman Fengler—editor of " Kurier Poznański " ; now member of the Polish National Council in London.

Dr. Stanisław Celichowski—Mayor of Poznań, a member of the Political Committee of the Party ; now in London.

Stanisław Grabski—a former leader of the Party ; until recently chairman of the Polish National Council.

Here is a list of *Zionist* leaders :

Dr. Yehoshua Gottlib—editor of the " Moment " a former Seym deputy and member of the highest Zionist Party authorities ; died in prison.

Józef Czernichów—chairman of the Vilno Jewish Community ; shot without trial at Wilejka prison during the evacuation of the prison in 1941.

Salomon Leder—a member of the Zionist Executive at Lvov ; fate unknown.

Mojżesz Reich—a member of the Executive Committee of the Misrakhi of Poland (a conservative-religious Zionist organisation) ; fate unknown.

Dr. Michael Ringe—a former member of the Senate from Lvov.

Aron Cincinnatus—a member of the Executive Committee at Vilno.

Aleksander and *Bolesław Ołomucki*—from the Warsaw Zionist Organisation.

A few non-Zionist Jewish leaders may be added :

Dr. Mojżesz Schorr—a professor of Warsaw University (oriental studies) ; a member of the Senate and of the Jewish Agency ; died in prison.

Wiktor Chajes—vice-mayor of the city of Lvov ; fate unknown.

Zelman Reizin—a member of the teaching staff of the Jewish Institute at Vilno and a prominent expert on the Yiddish language ; died in prison.

Natan Szwalbe—editor of a Jewish daily paper, published in Polish in Warsaw ('' Our Review '') ; fate unknown.

Saul Wagman—another editor of '' Our Review '' ; fate unknown.

Amongst others the following *Ukrainian National Democrat leaders* were arrested and deported :

Dymitr Levicky—a member of the Senate ; chairman of the Party ; died after release from prison.

Ostap Lucky—a Seym deputy ; fate unknown.

Nicholas Malicky—a member of the Senate ; most probably shot.

Volodimir Celevich—a Seym deputy ; most probably shot.

Volodimir Kuzmovich—a Seym deputy ; most probably shot.

Dimitr Velykanovich—a Seym deputy ; most probably shot.

H. Tarnavsky—a Seym deputy ; fate unknown.

H. Tershakovets—s Seym deputy ; fate unknown.

The names quoted above are but *a modest* sample of the many thousands of arrested and deported leaders.

When the political field had thus been swept clean, the authorities felt they could now proceed to stage elections which would enable the U.S.S.R. to claim popular support for their conquest of Eastern Poland.*

---

* The purge of poli ical and trades' union leaders was soon followed by mass deportation to the depths of the U.S.S.R. It is estimated that up to 1,500,000 people were deported during the 1939-1941 period of Soviet rule in Eastern Poland, in that number were included 52 per cent. Poles, 30 per cent. Jews, and 18 per cent. Ukrainians and white Ruthenians (Byelorussians). 59·2 per cent. of the deportees were workers, tradesmen, farmers and members of the forestry service. Thus half of the deportees belonged to the poorest class which the Soviet régime was to liberate from capitalist oppression and bestow with freedom and property. The other groups were: soldiers, 8 per cent. ; judges, 8 per cent ; clergymen of all creeds, professors, members of the university teaching staff, total 1·1 per cent. ; lawyers and engineers, 6 per cent. ; secondary and elementary school teachers, 4 per cent. ; and 20·9 per cent. other small groups.

The "Government" which the Soviet armies invading Poland in 1920 hoped to impose on the conquered country. Its leading members were: Marchlewski (6), Dzierżynski (5)—the future chief of the notorious GPU, and Kon (7). The character of the "Government" prepared for Poland in 1920 bore a striking similarity to that of the Lublin Committee of 1944.

Wanda Wasilewska

Edward Osubka-Morawski — Premier and Foreign Minister

CHAPTER VI

" FREE ELECTION " OR " SWINDLE DEMOCRACY " ?

The idea of " elections " or " plebiscite " did not arise at once.

After the hasty conclusion of the Partition Treaty of September 28th, 1939, the Nazi and the Soviet Governments directed an appeal to France and Britain urging them to cease hostilities against Germany, to conclude ' peace and to acquiesce in the partition of Poland :

> " When the German Government and the Govern-ment of the U.S.S.R. by their agreement signed today had finally settled the questions which remained as a result of the collapse of the Polish State, and have thereby created a strong foundation for lasting peace in Eastern Europe—*Pravda* wrote on September 29th—they put forward the view, in mutual understanding, that the liquidation of the present war between Germany on the one hand and England and France on the other, would be to the interest of all nations. Accordingly both Governments will direct their efforts in common, if necessary in agreement with other friendly powers, to the speediest possible attainment of that end."

When, however, it became clear that all the three members of the anti-Nazi alliance, Britain, France, and Poland, the latter in exile and underground, would further continue to wage war, and would not acknowledge Nazi or Soviet posses-sion of Poland, the two occupying powers resorted to different tactics. Germany simply incorporated Western and Central Poland into the Reich. The Soviet Union proceeded some-what more subtly. It decided to stage elections in order to show the world that the conquest of Eastern Poland was in accordance with the will of the population. In other words, conquest was to be propped up by the authority of Democracy.

However, there was a slip at the outset. In the first days of October, Soviet Commanders of the Ukrainian and White Ruthenian (Byelorussian) Fronts, and their military councils, appointed the Regional Provisional Administration in the Provinces of " the Western Ukraine " (cf. "Free Ukraine," of October 4th, 1939), and " Western White Ruthenia " (Byelorussia). The administrators thus appointed were Soviet nationals, Red Army officers or Red Army political commissars. Those of them who stood at the head of the administration of the Lvov and Białystok Provinces, announced in the press their decisions to hold elections throughout the occupied territories to two National Assemblies, one at Lvov, representing the " Western Ukraine," the other at Bialystok, to represent " Western Byelorussia." The enactment signed by the Lvov Provisional Administration and published in the Red Standard, Lvov, issue of October 5th, 1939, confidently formulated these Soviet administrators' hope that the population " would express at the National Assembly the deep and unshakable will . . . to build a free, happy and ample existence jointly and indissolubly with the whole Ukrainian nation in the powerful family of the Soviet Union," and that " a Soviet régime would be established in our land." Similar hopes were expressed by the Soviet administrators of the Białystok Province.

The slip consisted in thus acknowledging that the initiative of the elections came not from the people of Eastern Poland but from the Red Army. It is quite understandable that Soviet propaganda sources later preferred to pass over in silence the fact that the expression of " free will " had been initiated by the conquering army, the more so as only a week or two before the same army had been involved in the bloodshed of invasion.

The same neglect of the principles of democracy was shown in setting up two main committees, one at Lvov, the other at Białystok, whose task it was to organise the elections.

These committees were so composed as to have a majority of members imported from the Soviet Union with no ties whatsoever with the electoral areas. The Lvov Committee for the " Western Ukraine " included seven Red Army or N.K.V.D. officers (Begma, Gorbatenko, Grulenko, Gryshchuk, Lukin, Matsko and Yeremenko), the chairman of the Supreme Soviet of the Ukrainian (Grechukha) and a Soviet-Ukrainian writer (Korneychuk—later to become the first Foreign Commissar of the Ukrainian S.S.R.), the total number of Committee members being 17 (cf. *Izvestia* of October 11th, 1939). Similarly, among the 12 members of the Białystok Committee for " Western Byelorussia " there were : the chairman of the Supreme Soviet of the Byelorussian S.S.R. (Natalevich), two deputies to the same Soviet (Grekova and Pankov) and —at least—three Red Army or N.K.V.D. officers (Gaysin, Karkeyev and Spasov), cf. *Pravda* of October 11th, 1939. Thus, the Committees were nothing but another organ of the occupying power.

While Soviet nationals constituted a majority on both the main electoral committees, there were also several Soviet dignitaries amongst the candidates to the two assemblies. Like the committee members, they came from remote parts of Russia, and were completely alien to the constituencies. According to *Pravda* of October 15th, 1939 the following persons stood as candidates for elections to the " Byelorussian " Assembly : Ponomarenko, member of the War Council of the Byelorussian Front, secretary of the Central Committee of the Communist Party of Byelorussia, General Kovalev, leader of the Byelorussian Front, and the already mentioned Gaysin. According to *Pravda* of October 19th, 1939, M. V. Molotov, Foreign Commissar of the U.S.S.R. and at that time head of its Government, and Marshal E. Voroshilov, were put forward at Krzemieniec as candidates for the " Western Ukrainian " Assembly. Amongst the members of the Presidium of the " Western Ukrainian " Assembly as mentioned in *Pravda* of October 25th, 1939, we find eleven undoubted Soviet officials.

The rest of the candidates were recruited from amongst local Communists, or, in default of such, and with a view to misleading the voters, from amongst local inhabitants not likely to resist Soviet directives. It was only exceptional that a Ukrainian lawyer, Vinnichenko by name, elected to the " Western Ukrainian " Assembly, should have dared to vote *against* the incorporation of the " Western Ukraine " into the U.S.S.R., for which inadvertent act he was later duly sentenced to eight years' imprisonment as an " enemy of the people."

It is surprising that Vinnichenko should ever have been elected, as the candidates were either appointed by Soviet administrators or approved at *ad hoc* meetings called by these administrators and firmly managed according to instructions brought from the U.S.S.R.

According to *Pravda* of October 25th, 1939, the number of constituencies in " Western Byelorussia " was 929, and in the " Western Ukraine " 1,495. There were only as many candidates put forward as there were constituencies, so that the poor elector was even deprived of the possibility of choosing from amongst the Soviet nationals, the Communists, or the amenables, the one he might have liked best, or disliked least.

The atmosphere in which the elections took place was the same atmosphere " of fear and constraint " which K. Gibberd finds so characteristic of the Soviet Union itself (cf. p. 61, Soviet Russia, published in February, 1942, by the Royal Institute of International Affairs). This was due to several factors. The mere presence of large contingents of Red Army troops (700,000 men, i.e., approximately one fully armed man to 18 inhabitants—men, women and children) was sufficient to inspire fear and to create an atmosphere of constraint. Let us not forget that this army both from the legal point of view and on account of its composition was entirely foreign to Eastern Poland. Moreover, it did not remain politically inactive. Quite the contrary. Many quotations from the Soviet press of the period may be adduced to show that Red Army men and officers—either of their own will or on instructions from above—acted as election agitators. '' Here with us all Red Army men and their leaders must be agitators ''—a Soviet Colonel reported to *Pravda* (issue of September 21st, 1939) from the town of Nowogródek. '' During the period of preparation for the election of delegates to the National Assembly of the '' Western Ukraine,'' said *Izvestia* in retrospect, February 2nd, 1940—'' thousands of soldiers and officers carried on widespread political work among the population. Agitator-soldiers were everywhere. . . . Red Army men . . . also helped to create electoral districts . . . and drew up the lists of electors.''

Much more disquieting were the sinister activities of the N.K.V.D., which was effecting arrests and deportations to Russia on a mass scale, ruthlessly pursuing its aim of eliminating undesirable Polish, Ukrainian, Jewish and White Ruthenian (Byelorussian) elements and of inspiring at the same time a dread of the Soviet occupation authorities. We have already spoken of this in a previous chapter.

As if that were not enough, armed Communist militias and professional Soviet agitators imported *en masse* from the U.S.S.R. used physical or moral compulsion to ensure maximum participation in the polls.

On the other hand, there was no possibility of any propaganda against such participation. Moreover, it had been made abundantly clear that abstention was not something to be risked lightheartedly.

According to official Soviet data 92.83 per cent. and 96.71 per cent. voters took part in the polls in the '' Western Ukraine '' and '' Western Byelorussia '' respectively, while 90.93 per cent. and 90.67 per cent. gave valid votes for the Soviet-sponsored candidates.

Even under such circumstances there was only a one-way issue to be decided by the Assemblies, namely, that of the inclusion of Eastern Poland in the U.S.S.R. There was no question of the " Western Ukraine " and " Western Byelorussia," (the name given by the Soviet Authorities to the Polish Eastern Provinces) remaining part of Poland. In that sense, even regardless of the character and the atmosphere of the elections, neither the voting by the people, nor the subsequent resolutions adopted by the two Assemblies, were a plebiscite, as is sometimes claimed in the world press.

About a week after the elections, which took place on October 22nd, the two Assemblies met, at Białystok and Lvov, to adopt resolutions requesting the Soviet Government to accept " Western Byelorussia " and the " Western Ukraine " into the fold of the Union (on October 29th and 27th, respectively). After adopting these resolutions, the two Assemblies disappeared for ever.

These sham elections, and the subsequent resolutions of the Assemblies—" swindle democracy " at its best—were to be used henceforth for the purpose of inducing world opinion into believing that the incorporation of Eastern Poland into the U.S.S.R. was the result of the practical application of the doctrines of political democracy.

Mundus vult decipi (the world is easily deceived), provided it is given something to sweeten the deceit. The Nazis had failed to do that. The Soviets, in accordance with their lip-service to political democracy, had not. Therein lay the sublety of the Soviet method of annexation as contrasted with the highway robbery of the Nazis.

PART II

CHAPTER VII

UNPOPULARITY OF COMMUNISM IN POLAND

The subjection of the rest of Poland at some future date required in the first place that the number of Communist sympathisers should be adequately increased and their ranks strengthened. Here the Soviet leaders were presented with a difficult problem : on one hand, the Communist Party of Poland had ceased to exist as from 1937 : on the other, Communism was decidedly not popular with the peasants, workers and the working intelligentsia of the Soviet Union's western neighbour.

This was reflected, though perhaps imperfectly, in the number of Communist Seym deputies : none in the Seym of 1919-1922 ; six in that of 1922-1924 ; seven in that of 1928-1930 and four in that of 1930-1935 ; i.e., 0 per cent., 1.4 per cent., 1.6 per cent. and 0.9 per cent. respectively.

There were many reasons for the unpopularity of Communism.

In their struggle for the soul of the nation, the Polish Communists had been greatly handicapped from the very outset. They had had to contend with a formidable and long-established opponent, the Polish Socialist Party. The P.P.S., as the Poles call it, had a long tradition, as it had been set up in 1892, in Paris, whereas the Communist Party of Poland was a comparatively recent creation. The P.P.S. had taken part in 1905 in a revolutionary upheaval which had shaken the former Tsarist Empire, resulting in the only liberalization of the regime that Russia has ever experienced in her long history. The P.P.S. had done a great deal to re-establish Polish independence in 1918, and to maintain it against foreign aggression, whereas the Polish Communists, joining hands with the aggressors, had endeavoured to strangle that self-same independence, thus alienating the Polish masses. The attempt made in 1920 to thrust upon Poland a government supported solely by foreign bayonets was well remembered.

The P.P.S. belonged to the Second International, a free association of Socialist parties all over the world on a national basis, of which the British Labour Party is also a member, whereas the Communist Party of Poland, in actual fact, was only a territorial section of the Third International, directed from Moscow. The Socialists' record included many legislative measures to improve the lot of the Polish worker, whereas the Communists, always a negligible minority, had had no chance whatsoever of carrying anything through any of the legislative bodies in Poland. The P.P.S. were not aiming at abolishing private ownership of land, which is the aim of Communism everywhere. This was sufficient to make the Communists unpopular with the land-owning peasant of Poland with his deep-rooted attachment to his own strip of land. The Communists' hostility towards religion and religious practice, in contrast to the Socialists' toleration, also caused Communism to be thoroughly disliked in a country where religion is still a vivid force with many.

The unpopularity of Communism with the workers, the peasants and the working intelligentsia of Poland, led to numerous disputes within the Party concerning the problems of tactics and approach. The disputes led in turn to incessant rifts and mutual distrust. These were only enhanced by clashes between those of the Stalinite persuasion and the Trotskyites, engendered by the great conflict within the U.S.S.R. A disastrous situation arose in the Party, and, in 1937, the Komintern felt itself forced to decree its dissolution.

Thus in the autumn of 1939, when the incorporation of Eastern Poland into the U.S.S.R. was completed, there was in Poland no organised Communist Party which might have served the Communist Party of the Soviet Union as a tool for the further subjection of Western and Central Poland.

Nor was it easy to form such a party. Enmity towards Communism had only increased as a result of Soviet participation in the destruction of the Polish State in 1939, the misery and unhappiness thus brought about, and the population's experience of the blessings of the Soviet regime in Eastern Poland. On the other hand, the mutual suspicion and embitterment caused by the previous disputes and rifts within the Party, and also by its dissolution, had by no means been dispelled, so that much care and vigilance had to be applied in selecting candidates and forming them into a reliable hierarchy.

Therefore the re-creation of the Communist Party of Poland had to be deferred to a later date. For the time being, suitable men and women were to be selected as prospective candidates to the Party.

CHAPTER VIII

RECRUITING WRITERS

Two groups of society were given special attention : writers and officers. This choice was determined by the role of propaganda on the one hand, and armed force on the other, in bringing about revolution.

At first two associations were formed, an Alliance of Former Polish Communists and a Union of Former Political Prisoners. Next, a school for selecting writers was set up at Lvov in the form of a literary and political monthly called *New Horizons*, the first issue of which appeared in February, 1940, under the editorship of two ambitious and gifted women Communists, Helen Usiyevich and Wanda Wasilewska.

Helen Usiyevich was a daughter of a well-known Polish Communist, Feliks Kon, who, in the summer and autumn of 1920, was Premier-designate of the " Provisional Polish Revolutionary Government " prepared to assume power in Warsaw in the event of its capture by the Soviet armies. The period of 1920-1939 she had spent in Russia.

Wanda Wasilewska, a daughter of a distinguished Liberal, a close collaborator of Marshal Pilsudski's, had secretly embraced Communism long before the war, and had now revealed herself as a Communist by joining the Soviet Ukrainian Communist Party at Lvov.

Then, Mme. Wasilewska remembered her young daughter left back in Warsaw. We are in a position to give an interesting quotation from the memoirs of someone who witnessed the following scene at Lvov :

" Several weeks after the tragic and dreary September, when whole Poland grieved over fathers, sons, husbands and brothers, fallen in battle, and when the Gestapo raged throughout the conquered country and, at night, dragged from their dwellings many Polish writers and officers, soldiers and students, peasants and workers, an elegant brand new car pulled up at the gate of a house in Lvov, then occupied by the Red Army, and was soon followed by a big lorry. From the car emerged two genuine Gestapo agents, and—to the passers-by astonishment—led out of the car a beautiful, ashen-haired, and very young girl whom they handed over to a tall and slightly too corpulent lady. Then workers began to unload the lorry and to carry the furniture it contained into the lady's house

" This tall and corpulent lady was Wanda Wasilewska. The beautiful ashen-haired lass, brought by the Gestapo agents in the elegant car, was her daughter Eva, who, in virtue of an official arrangement between the Soviet and the Nazi authorities had been brought from the Nazi-occupied Warsaw to her mother at Lvov. The furniture was that of the lady's Warsaw flat. The Gestapo agents carried out their mission, saluted, and drove off back to Warsaw, to their work. To their " wet " work. They drove off to bring similar beautiful ashen-haired and very young girls not to their mothers but to German concentration camps or to German brothels. They drove off to deport the daughters of unprivileged Polish parents, fighting against the Nazis, without compromise."

The two women gained the collaboration of other Communist writers, the poet Jerzy Putrament, of Vilno, a recent convert as in his student days he was an active and unpleasant Jew-baiter, Jerzy Borejsza (Goldman),* Alfred Lampe† and A. Ważyk (Wagman). Difficult living conditions, the fear of persecution by the Soviet authorities (on 23rd January, 1940, several Left Wing writers had been arrested and deported to Russia, such as the poet Broniewski, A. Stern, T. Parnicki and A. Wat), and perhaps a desperate and misconceived attempt to adapt their liberal socialist views to the harsh realities of Sovietism, led several writers to somewhat reluctant collaboration on the journal. However, in the long run, these new adepts did not prove good acquisitions for the political purposes pursued by the *New Horizons* school. Some of them, as for instance the talented translator of masterpieces of French literature into Polish, the indomitable fighter for progress, T. Boy-Zelenski deliberately stayed in Lvov after its capture by the Nazis in the early summer of 1941, only to be shot by them later in the same year.

Nevertheless, some, as for example E. Szemplinska and L. Szenwald, left Lvov for the Soviet Union and identified themselves with the Soviet cause.

Let us add that the publication of *New Horizons* was stopped in June, 1941, as a result of the Nazi attack on the Soviet Union and an early capture of Lvov.

For some time, the Soviet authorities seemed to have abandoned the idea of publishing the organ. However, when the fortunes of war improved, *New Horizons* was restarted at Kuybyshev, on May 5th, 1942, this time as a fortnightly, about two months before the evacuation of the

* When the Communist Party of Poland still existed, Borejsza-Goldman belonged to the Stalinite section within it. Therefore he enjoyed special Soviet confidence even after the dissolution of the Party. He was mainly responsible for the arrest and deportation of Broniewski and other Left Wing writers. At the present time Borejsza is Editor-in-Chief of the two daily papers published in Lublin, *Rzeczpospolita* and *Gazeta Polska*.

† Alfred Lampe (died on 10th December, 1943, in Moscow) was a member of the Polish Communist Government of the summer of 1920. He was one of the most prominent Komintern agents in Poland, was reputed to have been the brain behind " New Horizons " and, later, the " Union of Polish Patriots."

Polish Army from the U.S.S.R. to the Middle East. If we mention this coincidence of dates, it is only because our fortnightly was to discharge at a later date, the mission of making public the plan of forming a Soviet-Polish Army on Soviet soil.

CHAPTER IX

VILLA OF BLISS

As a result of the Soviet occupation of Eastern Poland, 181,000 officers and men were alleged to have been taken prisoner by the Red Army (cf. the figures published in the Red Army paper, *The Red Star* issue of September 17th, 1940).

The prisoners were subjected to intensive Communist propaganda which was, however, successfully counteracted by the misery of the Soviet masses which the prisoners had ample opportunity to observe and by the harsh treatment they received from camp commanders and guards.

However, in the autumn of 1940, after a year of propaganda skilfully exploiting the seeds of disillusion sown by the Polish military defeat of 1939, a certain number of officers of various grades allowed themselves to be persuaded that the only future open to Poland was to become a Soviet republic, that no faith was to be placed in '' perfidious Albion '' and her "credulous agent" the Sikorski Government in London.

These officers were assembled by the N.K.V.D. at Malakhovka, in a villa that they came to call '' the Villa of Bliss '' owing to the unexpectedly good conditions there. They had come from dreary prisoner-of-war camps, with little food and with lice swarming. Now they found themselves in a clean house, surrounded by a pine-wood. True, the place was under close observation, but the agents were well trained, and did their best to efface themselves. The rooms were comfort itself. A well stocked library, wireless sets, plenty of cigarettes, unrestricted correspondence with relatives and friends back in Poland, pretty coquettish chambermaids, choice food—all this, after months of prison-camp life, made a deep impression on the officers.

Here the prospective leaders of the Soviet Polish Army were educated in the Soviet Communist gospel, and in tactical problems such as street fighting, seizing power by revolution etc. Their leader was Zygmunt Berling, then a lieutenant-colonel who was later to become the C.-in-C. of the Soviet-Polish Army in the U.S.S.R.

After the completion of the course, those officers who satisfied the political requirements of the N.K.V.D., 74 in number, signed a formula of loyalty to the U.S.S.R.

Since, according to the *Red Star* issue quoted above, there were in Soviet captivity 9,369 Polish officers,* the meagre result achieved by the Soviet authorities is in itself striking testimony of the truth. Black sheep may be found any-where, especially in conditions of national disaster. The relevant fact is their number in relation to the whole. The proportion was 74 in 9,369.

CHAPTER X

THE NAZIS ATTACK

The Second World War had already lasted for about a year. The Soviet-Nazi Non-Aggression Pact had had a similar duration.

As late as August 1st, 1940, M. Molotov spoke of " good neighbourly and friendly " Nazi-Soviet relations (cf. Soviet Peace Policy, p. 73). Nevertheless, already in the autumn of 1940, even the most cautious observers of the situation were beginning to admit that an armed conflict would break out between the two dynamic States within a measurable span of time.

---

* According to the Polish estimate about 15,000 active and reserve officers found themselves in Russia as a result of the events of 1939.

The storm broke on June 22nd, 1941, i.e., after some 21 months had elapsed since the joint partition of Poland.

The first month of the fighting was marked by a series of unbroken and spectacular Nazi successes. On June 29th, the outskirts of Minsk, capital of the Byelorussian S.S.R. were reached. On July 8th, Ostrov, east of the Latvian border, was taken. On July 11th, the Nazis were already on the Dnieper to the east of Minsk. On July 16th, they entered Smolensk in Byelorussia. On July 17th, they were at Kishinev (Bessarabia). On July 19th, Novogrod in Eastern Volhynia was in their hands.

In the latter half of July, 1941, in view of these Nazi victories, the question might have been asked in all fairness to what extent, and indeed, whether at all, the U.S.S.R. would be able to withstand the onslaught. It is impossible to know whether such doubts haunted the leaders of the Soviet Union at the time. It was, however, more than evident that the U.S.S.R. badly needed British and American help in the shape of armaments, ammunition and food. This need automatically brought up the issue of Polish-Soviet relations.

Poland was the country in whose defence Great Britain and France had taken up arms in September, 1939. She had a formal treaty of alliance with Great Britain (concluded on August 25th, 1939). In view of her loyalty and the services she had rendered to the common cause, Poland had some standing, not only with the British and Americans, but also with pro-Allied neutral opinion throughout the world. A reconciliation with Poland was therefore necessary from the point of view of Soviet relations with the prospective purveyors of armaments, i.e., Great Britain and America.

This, however, was not the only factor in favour of reconciliation. The Nazi attack on the Soviet Union had been quickly joined by the two European neighbours of the U.S.S.R., i.e., Finland (on June 25th, as a result of an attack by Soviet troops) and Rumania (on June 22nd) and by the near-neighbour States of Hungary (on June 27th) and Slovakia (on June 24th). The two former powers could claim reasons for their attack. They had been deprived respectively of the Karelian Isthmus (by the Soviet-Finnish peace treaty of March 12th, 1940), and of Northern Bukovina and Bessarabia (by the Soviet-enforced agreement of June 28th, 1940). Hungary and Slovakia had no such grievance as loss of valuable national territory to justify their participation in the war against the Soviet Union. In harmony with the behaviour of the four German satellites, the Soviet-held republic of Lithuania rose *en masse* against the retreating Red Army at the end of June, and a similar trend was only too evident among the Ukrainians, and also, though to a lesser extent, among the White Ruthenians (Byelorussians).

These facts could not but have increased Soviet interest in the behaviour of the Poles. The Soviet leaders knew only too well that they had alienated the Poles by forcibly incorporating—not slices of territory as in the case of Finland and Rumania—but over one-half of Poland into the Soviet Union. Deportations and other methods of Sovietisation had only increased bad feeling between the Poles and the Soviet. Consequently there was incomparably more inflammable material in Poland which the Nazis might have been able to exploit against the Soviet Union than in any of the four Nazi satellite States mentioned above. Poland's population amounted to a little more than that of these four countries put together. Strategically, as adjacent to the Reich, Polish territory was again more important than the territories of Finland, Hungary, Rumania and Slovakia.

These considerations, in the fateful July, 1941, constituted another imperative inducement for the Soviet leaders to bring about a reconciliation with the Polish Government, behind which stood firmly the whole of the Polish nation.

As for the Polish Government, its policy was that of loyalty to the Democracies and to the Polish-British mutual assistance pact of August 25th, 1939. The conclusion of a British-Soviet pact on July 12th, 1941, made it necessary, therefore, for Poland to seek a rapprochement with the Soviet Union.

The good offices of the British Government, and the efforts of the representatives of the two countries directly concerned, were crowned on July 30th, 1941, by the conclusion of a Polish-Soviet Agreement. The Agreement provided for recognition by the Soviet Government that the " Soviet-German Treaties of 1939 as to territorial changes in Poland have lost their validity." It restored diplomatic relations between the Soviet and the Polish Governments. Moreover, it expressed Soviet consent to the formation on Soviet soil of a " Polish Army under a Commander appointed by the Polish Government in agreement with the Soviet Government, the Polish Army on the territory of the U.S.S.R. being subordinated in an operational sense to the supreme command of the U.S.S.R. upon which the Polish Army will be represented." Last but not least, the agreement provided for a release of the Polish prisoners of war (taken by the Red Army in September, 1939), and of Polish citizens detained in the U.S.S.R. (arrested in Eastern Poland and deported thence during the two-year period of Soviet occupation).

By the agreement, the Soviet leaders again recognised the existence of an independent Polish State, and discarded the only pretext for international approval of their seizure of Eastern Poland.

As subsequent developments had demonstrated beyond any doubt, this was for them a harsh war-dictated necessity, and a retrograde step. They therefore did their best, under the prevailing circumstances, not to carry out the Agreement, and to reject it *de facto* as soon as the situation allowed.

Władisław Gomułka — Vice Premier

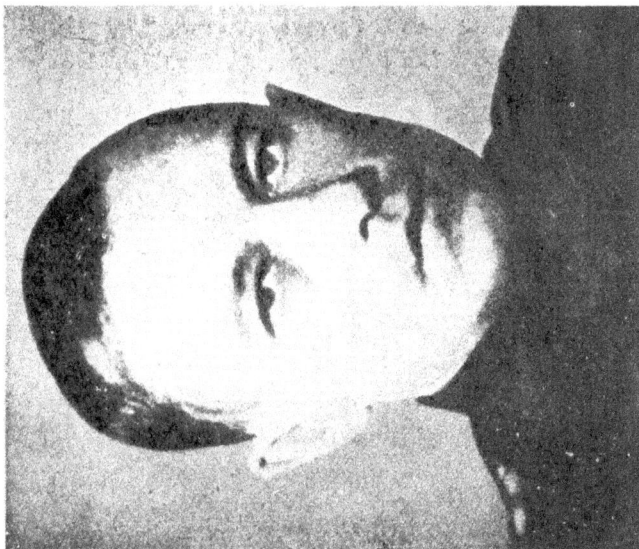

Jan Rabanowski — Minister of Communications

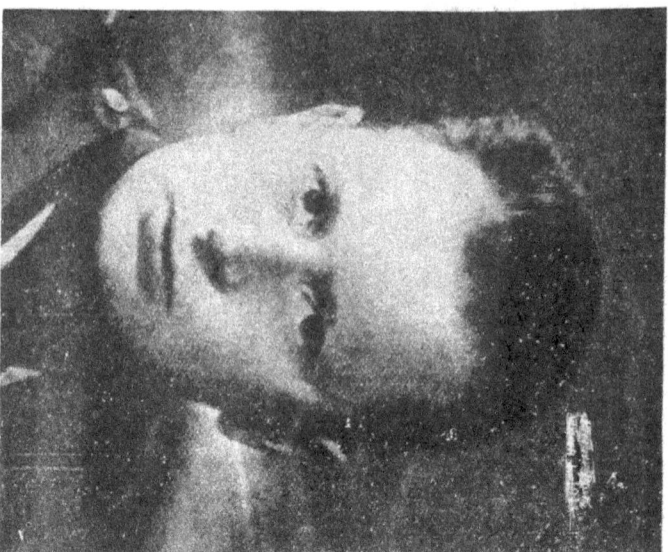

Stefan Matuszewski — Minister of Information

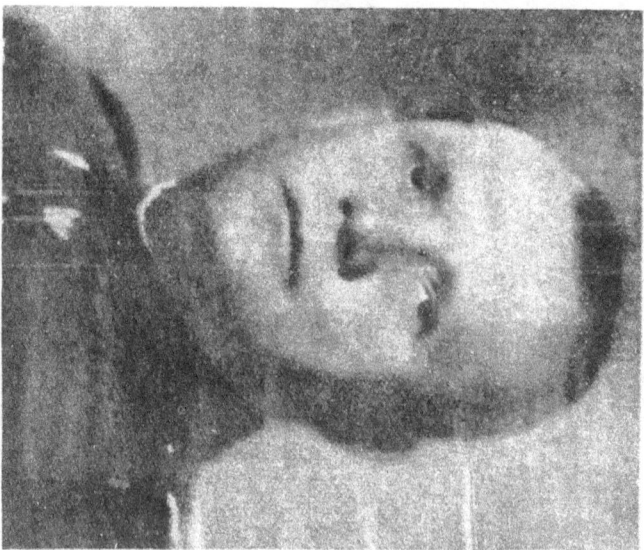

General Rola-Zymierski — Minister of Defence

Chapter XI

THE COMMUNIST PARTY OF POLAND
RESURRECTED

We have already dealt with the unpopularity of Communism in Poland, and with the dissolution in 1937 of the Communist Party of Poland by the Komintern.

In the winter of 1941/2 this party was reconstituted in the greatest secrecy by the same Komintern.

The moment chosen was that of the Red Army's first recovery from the shock inflicted by the series of defeats during the first half-year of the Nazi-Soviet war. The military situation was yet by no means re-established, and the reconstitution of the Party might well have seemed premature. However, further evolution of events proved that it was not so. In any case, the fact that the first possible opportunity was seized showed on one hand that the selection of candidates had borne fruit, and, on the other, that the Komintern leaders were only too eager to revert to their fixed policy of preparing the organisation of Poland on the Soviet model.

It would be unfair to allege that the existence of a Polish Communist Party infringed the letter or the spirit of the Polish-Soviet Agreement of July 30th, 1941. Far from it. The new Poland, as envisaged by true Polish leaders, will be democratic, and will certainly endeavour to live on the best of terms with its Communists—provided these do not attempt to seize power by force, as was recently the case in Greece. Nevertheless, in view of the specific Polish experience of 1919-1920, and of the events following the outbreak of the present war, this issue was and is rather delicate.

The Communist Party of Poland was re-established under the name of the Polish Workers' Party. The reason for not naming it the Communist Party was a tactical one : as we have already pointed out, Communism was not popular with the working population or the intelligentsia of Poland, and neither the two-year occupation of Eastern Poland nor the personal experience of the Soviet regime by the hundreds of thousands of deportees and prisoners had tended to increase its popularity. Therefore both the Polish Communists and their Soviet preceptors preferred to act under the camouflage of the name " Polish Workers' Party "*. Only careful and systematic readers of the *Kommunisticheskiy Internatsional* (" The Communist International," i.e., the Komintern) could have obtained definite proof of the Workers' Party being nothing else but the Communist Party in disguise. To wit, when the dissolution of the Komintern was decided upon, on May 15th, 1943, its organ gave in its last issue, No. 5-6, 1943 cf. pp. 12-25, the resolutions of the various Communist Parties of the world loyally approving the step taken by the Presidium of the Komintern. There, on page 19, the resolution of the Polish Workers' Party is to be found inserted between those of the Communist Party of Hungary and the Communist Party of Switzerland.

Among the founders of the Polish Workers' Party were four experienced Komintern agents of Polish birth : Bierut, the recently appointed " President " of Poland, Kazimierz Hardy, Kulesza-Lutomski and Kwiatkowska. A year later, a Political Bureau of the Party was set up, with the participation of the already mentioned Bierut, of Stanislaw Kotek-Agroszewski, later at the head of the Department of Public Administration of the Polish Committee of National Liberation, Szymon Zolna, later a member of the National Council of the Homeland.

The chief aim of the newly recreated Party was to set up cells with a view to providing a skeleton machinery for seizing power in Poland in the future. The Communists, therefore, did their best to infiltrate into the Polish Underground Movement without, however, revealing their political identity, and endeavoured to discover the structure of the organisation and

---

* " Polska Partia Robotnicza " in Polish, or P.P.R. in abbreviation. This was quickly given the ironic interpretation of " Płaceni Przez Rosję " (i.e., " paid by Russia ") by the Polish Underground Movement.

its leaders. Aided by agents dropped by parachute from the Soviet Union, they organised groups, mostly in forests or in localities far away from towns, roads and communications lines, which then adopted a " wait-and-see " policy, whilst receiving world-wide publicity from Soviet propaganda as allegedly fighting the Nazi invader. These groups were styled " The People's Guard " or " The People's Army," and were conceived as military cells reserved for future action.

At first the Underground Movement tended to disregard the existence and the activities of the re-born Communist Party. Communism—it was argued, was far from ever becoming popular. As to the U.S.S.R.—it was believed—the Communist State was no longer really interested in spreading its doctrine abroad and thus causing friction and dissatisfaction.

When, however, facts gave ample and conclusive proof that the Polish Communists were aiming at seizing power for themselves, the Polish Underground Press, felt compelled to unmask them.

We give here two quotations from a Peasant Party Underground organ and a Socialist organ :

" The Communists carry on their activities in Poland on several levels. They present themselves under different names, never under their own. They use a whole host of slogans, calculated to gain the support of many different groups of our society. Their main organisation has been named ' The Polish Workers' Party ' ; their militia ' The People's Guard.' Apart from that, they are trying to piece together a new species of ' popular front ' which they have named ' The People's Army.' They are aided by a ' Polish Workers' Socialist Party,' and are trying to set up a ' radical peasant party ' with the help of some former deputies who, in 1935, after an unsuccessful attempt to split the Peasant Party, went over to the O.Z.N.' (the mainstay of the Colonels' regime in pre-war Poland.)

" Both the ' Polish Workers' Party ' and its ' People's Army ' are careful to avoid the use of their own name of

Communists in their activities. In their hypocrisy and mendacity they are making exaggerated use of patriotic and independentist phraseology, thus endeavouring to conceal their true role and their treacherous aims

'' The Polish peasantry will not let itself be deluded by the misleading programme of ' radical reforms ' in the style of State Socialism modelled on that of Russia. They do not want to become manorial serfs in the barracks of the collective farms, or slave workers in the hands of state bureaucracy. The programme of the Polish Peasant Movement and the ways and means leading to its realisation are totally different from the aims and tactics of Communism. The struggle we are waging against them is ideological in character, and is determined by the moral principles that should prevail in life and in battle. The differences are profound and irreconcilable. We are concerned not only with whether the peasant is to have a holding of his own, a house and a cow, but also with whether he is to have freedom, free will and his own human dignity. Here we touch on the essence of things, their deepest sense. We are concerned with the human being, and that that human being should be himself, a thinking and feeling being, and not a spiritual dwarf or slave.

'' Under the Communist, as under the Nazi-Fascist regime, there is no individual, no human being. There is a mass shaped in one mould and to one pattern. There is the huge state machinery, and there are little cogs, screws, nuts and bolts—society. All that is harnessed together, pressed into one rhythm, into the same drive. It has been called ' dictatorship of the proletariat.' This is at once nonsense and imposture. Dictatorship can only be the rule of a minority (a clique, a caste or a class) over the majority, i.e., society, never the contrary. The proletariat constitutes a huge majority of the population of a State, and if there is a dictatorship, the proletariat does not rule, but is ruled by someone else. This some-one is represented by the Party bosses, the elite, a new caste of upstart magnates. We have created for ourselves an ideal of man's freedom entirely different from the Soviet conception, a different conception of the free creator of the common weal. We have declared war to throw off the yoke of capitalism, not with the aim of becoming a mass deprived of will and a victim to the State-Moloch which would devour everybody and everything.

" Anyhow, no action of the German criminals, directed against the Communists or the Soviet parachutist saboteurs, can receive any support from us, nor evoke any friendly feeling. . . . Our rifles and bombs are now directed only against the Germans."—(From *Through Struggle Towards Freedom*, an underground organ of the Peasant Party, issue of November 28th, 1943, Warsaw).

This is what the Socialists had to say about the " Polish Workers' Party " :

" Betrayal of Poland—this is the only qualification for the Communist plans now revealed. . . . It will only crown the shameful role which the Communists played before. Then they wrecked the unity of the workers' movement. Today they want to disrupt Poland from within, so that she may fall a prey to Russia. This work is so obvious that no one in Poland will allow himself to be deceived. The calculation is based on the weariness and the exhaustion of the continuously bleeding masses. . . . The Communists . . . must be isolated . . . so as to leave no doubt whatsoever that the whole Polish people backs its Government. Only the Polish Government has the right to represent Poland abroad. It has the organised backing of worker, peasant and intellectual. Only the Polish Government and its organs can organise and direct the political and military struggle aiming at the overthrow of Hitlerite might and the reconstruction of the Polish State."—(From *The Worker in Struggle*, January 9th, 1944, a Socialist underground organ in Warsaw).

The two organs of the Polish Underground Left Wing faithfully reflected the mood of the Polish masses towards the machinations of the fanatics of the creed so utterly alien to Poland.

However, the fanatics continued their subversive work and foreign support was not lacking.

Chapter XII

ON KOMINTERN WAVELENGTH

As long as Nazi-Soviet relations were good, the Komintern did not do anything to disturb them. Quite the contrary— Communist papers all over the world were full of anti-war propaganda, and the London *Daily Worker* even had to be suspended for its persistent endeavours to undermine the morale of the British working class.

Similarly, no propaganda came from Soviet territory to encourage the Poles engaged in struggle against the Nazi oppressor of Central and Western Poland. Not that they would have needed it or heeded it.

The outbreak of Soviet-Nazi war brought about a radical and instantaneous change of line in Communist propaganda.

Several months after it, late in the autumn of 1941, just before the Communist Party of Poland was re-established, the Komintern also organised a broadcasting Station, which, using good Polish, began to expatiate on Polish problems. The name it took was that of a greatly revered Polish national hero, General Tadeusz Kosciuszko, also known in the United States where he had taken part in the War of Independence.

A Polish Communist, Jakub Billig by name, stood at the head of the Station.

Before the war, Billig had worked in an Italian Insurance Company in Warsaw. At the same time he acted as an agent for the Communist M.O.P.R. (International Organisation of Aid for the Workers) and wasted much effort in attempts to organise Communist cells in the Polish Army.

Whilst the Kosciuszko Station made no bones about the necessity for the incorporation to the Soviet Union of Eastern Poland, though this was clouded in beautiful phraseology of Democracy and Brotherhood, at first it was rather diplomatic towards the Polish Government and the party coalition around it.

Less diplomatic it was in regard to matters of Polish policy, since without consulting any Polish official quarters, it tried to provoke the Polish nation into a premature mass uprising against the Nazis. E.g., on February 17th, 1942, the Komintern Station broadcast the following appeal :

" This is the third year of the Polish nation's struggle against the cruel invader. During this struggle many Poles have given proof of unheard of heroism, of tremendous self-denial and of readiness for sacrifice for the beloved fatherland. Polish patriots' deeds have undoubtedly wrought much damage to the Hitlerites, however, the results achieved are insignificant in comparison with the strength and supplies of the enemy. These results also are disproportionate in comparison with the possibilities at the disposal of the Polish nation situated as it is in the hinterland of the German front. These possibilities are only enhanced by the victories of the Red Army, due to which the battlefield is coming nearer to the Polish nation. Therefore, the Polish nation ought to reject at once all recipes that recommend waiting until the appropriate moment. The Polish guerilla detachments ought to operate not in small detachments, but in thousands. Millions ought to take part in guerilla fighting, with the Polish working class in the first ranks of the fighters."

At the time of this and such-like appeals, in the winter of 1941-2, the Soviet armies were still very far away, engaged in hard, insecure, and mostly defensive fighting, and any mass uprising in Poland could have resulted in nothing else but widespread massacre of Polish fighters and very small gain indeed for the common cause.

Although the Soviet authorities had, without any foundation, rejected the request of the Polish Embassy that Poles forcibly enrolled into the German Army, and taken prisoner by the Soviets, should be handed over to the Polish military authorities in the U.S.S.R. to join the ranks of the Polish Army, the Kosciuszko Station regularly assured these who had become German soldiers against their own will, that they would be able to join the Polish Army (e.g., broadcast of February 18th, 1942). Only afterwards it became clear what " Polish " Army the Communists had in mind already at that time.

From time to time, clear threads of veiled Communist propaganda could be detected in the Kosciuszko broadcasts, which had been conceived, *inter alia*, as help for the activities of the then recently re-born Communist Party of Poland. Thus, e.g., on February 27th, 1942, the Station appealed to the nation to set up workers' and peasants' committees. Anyone acquainted with the role of those committees during the Bolshevik Revolution could easily have divined what they could mean for Poland.

Otherwise the station, in accordance with its name, was ultra-patriotic, with all the noisy and pompous pseudo-patriotic phraseology apparently intended to conceal the station's true aim.

Taking into account the vivid religious sentiment of the Polish masses, only enhanced by the bestial persecution of the Nazis, the station was very religious, very Christian and even very Catholic. At times, it might even have appeared to be " plus catholique que le Pape " and based on the principle that Poland " was worth a Mass."

After the first period of correctness towards the Polish Government and the Polish democratic parties streams of criticism began to pour on the station's wavelength. The abuse of Polish official and political circles took a second place only to that allotted to fulsome praise, merited and unmerited, of the Soviet Union and its policies.

When in May, 1943, the Komintern was dissolved, which step, as one might have noticed since has not changed the policy of any single Communist party in the world by one iota, the Kosciuszko Station did not disappear from the air.

In the summer of 1944 it became responsible for one of the two broadcasts calling upon the people of Warsaw to rise against the Germans.

On August 22nd, 1944, the station closed down, recommending to its listeners the newly established broadcasting station of the Lublin Committee which thus acquired Komintern tradition.

CHAPTER XIII

SIKORSKI'S DREAM

In Article 4 of the Polish-Soviet Agreement of July 30th, 1941, the Soviet Government had expressed " its consent to the formation on the territory of the Union of Soviet Socialist Republics of a Polish Army."

On August 14th, 1941, a supplementary Polish-Soviet Military Agreement was signed which, *inter alia*, stipulated that this army was to " form part of the armed forces of the sovereign Republic of Poland " (Article 2, paragraph (*a*)). According to Article 6, " officers and other ranks " were to " be called from among Polish citizens on the territory of the U.S.S.R. by conscription and voluntary enlistment."

The late General Sikorski, whose dream it was to effect a *lasting* Polish-Soviet reconciliation, expected that on the strength of the two Agreements it would be possible to raise an army of at least 300,000 men. His calculation was even perhaps too conservative. According to the Red Army paper, *Krasnaya Zvezda* (*The Red Star*), issue of 18th September, 1940, there had been at that time in the U.S.S.R. 181,000 Polish prisoners of war. Moreover, about 100,000 Polish nationals were serving with the Red Army as a result of Soviet conscription in the spring of 1941. Lastly, there were in various parts of the U.S.S.R. about 1,500,000 Polish nationals of all ages and both sexes forcibly deported or sent to places of detention there. Neither of the two agreements stipulated any limitation of the strength of the proposed army.

A force of over 300,000 would have greatly increased Poland's participation in the common struggle against Nazi Germany. At the same time, it would have considerably strengthened

Poland's position among the United Nations. This was not anticipated in the plans of the U.S.S.R. However, a Soviet-Polish army suited them very well.

Various means were devised by the Soviet authorities to whittle down the proposed number to something like 75,000, i.e., 25 per cent. of the figure which Sikorski envisaged. As early as November 6th, 1941, difficulties in supplying food and equipment were alleged. December, 1941, saw unilateral restrictions of conscription and recruitment of volunteers to Poles only, to the exclusion of Polish citizens of Ukrainian, White Ruthenian and Jewish origin. Later on, Soviet members of the draft boards did their best to hamper enrolment. Almost none of the Polish nationals—Poles or non-Poles—who had been conscripted in Eastern Poland in 1941 were allowed to transfer to the Polish Army. In 1941, a ban was placed on the sale of railway tickets to Polish nationals, who were thus prevented from reaching the Polish military camps. In March, 1942, recruitment and voluntary enlistment for the Polish Army were stopped altogether.

Towards the end of June, 1942, the Soviet Government advised the British Ambassador in Moscow of its desire that the Polish Army should be moved from the U.S.S.R. to the Middle East. As a result, the Polish Army, then numbering 42,000 men, joined its British and Polish comrades in the Middle East. About 33,000 had been evacuated earlier in accordance with the Agreement of 14th August, 1941.

In this way, the terrain was cleared for the formation of a Soviet-Polish Army, with a view to which officers had been selected as early as 1940, and which had only been temporarily suspended during the period of the worst Soviet setbacks in the war against the Nazi invader.

Sikorski's dream was shattered. It had been a dream of someone who always refused to believe in organised bad faith.

CHAPTER XIV

UNDER THE PATRIOT BANNER

Even under its camouflaged name of " Polish Workers' Party," the Communist Party of Poland was not a suitable organisation to be presented to the Polish nation as an alternative to the coalition of democratic parties which constitutes the backbone of the Polish Government.

Something different had to be found, more palatable and at the same time as little suggestive as possible of Communism. This was the idea behind the emergence on March 1st, 1943, of a Union of Polish Patriots, presided over by het already mentioned woman Communist, Wanda Wasilewska. On that day, a weekly was started in Moscow under the name of *Wolna Polska* (*Free Poland*), as the organ of the Union.

The word " patriot " has a peculiar ring in Polish. The reason for this is that since the liquidation of ancient Poland in 1795 until its re-emergence in 1918, the Polish nation had lived under abnormal conditions. As a result, a whole vocabulary of ultrasentimental words and expressions developed, which differed from that of countries with a more normal evolution, perhaps not in essence, but decidedly in emotional value. The wolf's sheepskin was thus badly chosen, and, although the wolf was no less dangerous for that, down-trodden Poland had a hearty laugh when it first heard of the Union's name.

As already mentioned, the Union came into existence on March 1st, 1943. The Soviet Government's severance of diplomatic relations with the Polish Government occurred just over six weeks later. As the reader may remember, the Soviet Government tried to justify the severance of relations by alleging offence at the Polish Government's stand in the tragic Katyn affair. Let us therefore recall in brief the main elements of that unhappy occurrence.

On April 12th, 1943, the Nazis first published data concerning a mass grave of Polish officers in Katyn Forest, near Smolensk, Byelorussia. Naturally enough, they alleged that the officers, several thousand in number, who had been captured by the Red Army in September, 1939, had been murdered by the N.K.V.D. in the spring of 1940*. Naturally enough again, the Soviets rejected the Nazi accusation by alleging that the Nazis themselves were the murderers, and that the mass murder had been committed in the autumn of 1941, the number of victims being 11,000 (cf. " The Truth About Katyn, Report of a Special Commission for Ascertaining and Investigating the Circumstances of the Shooting of Polish Officer Prisoners by the German Fascist Invaders in the Katyn Forest," p. 12, supplement to the *Soviet War News Weekly*, undated). Both versions confirmed what was the essential fact for the Polish nation : several thousand Polish officers, enough to set up a powerful army, had been killed in captivity.

It may be argued, and not without justification, that, after hearing this appalling news, the Polish Government, which had vainly been endeavouring to trace the missing officers since October, 1941, should not have addressed itself to the International Red Cross with a request to undertake investigations. For not only does the U.S.S.R. Red Cross not belong to the International Red Cross, but a request directed to that body was liable to the misinterpretation that the Polish Government was hesitating between the two versions of the mass murder, instead of instantaneously embracing the Soviet version. Calm detachment in the face of the cold-blooded murder of thousands of Polish manhood was certainly the only advisable attitude. However it might have been, the Soviet Government promptly seized upon this

---

* Amtliches Material zum Massenmord von Katyn, im Auftrage des Auswartigen Amtes auf Grund urkundlichen Beweissmaterials zusammengestellt, bearbeitet und herausgegeben von der Deutschen Informationsstelle, Gedruckt in Deutschen Verlag, Berlin, 1943, gives list of 4,143 corpses identified up to June 7th, 1943.

opportunity to declare, on April 25th, 1943, that, in view of the behaviour of the Polish Government, they were severing diplomatic relations with Poland.

The real reason for this regrettable step was the fixed policy of the U.S.S.R. The Katyn affair was nothing but a pretext. Since the victory at Stalingrad, the scales of war had decisively turned in favour of the Soviet Union, and the long-established policy could be resumed more openly than before.

The Polish-Soviet Military Agreement had been fulfilled by the Soviet Government only in part. The Polish Army had been evacuated over nine months before (since 1943 it has been fighting in Italy). The idea of creating a Soviet-Polish Army had been put forward publicly some three months before, by a Soviet agent, with whom we deal later. It had been taken up two months before by a wider agency, the Union of Patriots, which at the same time presented its claim to act on behalf of the whole Polish nation, which privilege and burden is usually reserved for the legal Government.

Wanda Wasilewska, chairman of the Union, had undoubtedly become a good *Soviet* patriot during the war. This is what her closest associate, Helen Usiyevich, co-editor. of *New Horizons* had to say about her in a pamphlet published in 1941 by the State Publishing firm Khudozhestvennaya Literature in Moscow, under the title " Wanda Wasilewska."

> " The Soviet frontier—according to the picturesque expression of Wanda Wasilewska—came forward to thousands of people among whom was also the writer, breaking through to the east with the last of her strength, to the land of Socialism, to the great fatherland of all workers."—(P. 42, the author has in mind the entry of the Red Army into Poland on September 17th, 1939, a day tragic for every Pole.)

> " It was no wonder that when Wasilewska came to the Soviet Union "she was met as our own Soviet writer."—(P. 63.)

" Later on, Wasilewska was ' elected ' to the Supreme Soviet of the Soviet Union at Lvov."—(P. 63.)

" From the very first moment of her arrival in the Socialist Fatherland, Wanda Wasilewska felt at home, on native soil, a fighter among other fighters for Socialism."—(P. 63.)

" Her articles in *Pravda, Izvestia, Krasnaya Zvezda* (*The Red Star*, organ of the Red Army), and in several other Soviet papers, are a beautiful example of revolutionary political writing."—(P. 63.)

" Soviet literature was presented, in the person of Wanda Wasilewska, with a most beautiful talent." (P. 64.)

We have little to add to the information and eulogies of such an authority as Helen Usiyevich, the more so as her pamphlet was published by the State Publishing Firm, though no other course is open to anyone in the Soviet Union. One detail, however, may be of interest : after the death at Lvov in the autumn of 1939 of Wasilewska's second husband, Marian Bogatko*, this woman member of the Soviet Ukrainian Communist Party was happily married to a talented Soviet-Ukrainian writer, Körneychouk, who was to become in 1944 the First Commissar for Foreign Affairs of the Ukrainian S.S.R. Thus, even if we leave out of account her voluntary resignation of Polish nationality in allowing herself to be elected to the Supreme Soviet of the U.S.S.R., and in accepting the appointment to the rank of colonel in the Red Army, her marriage to a foreigner would have involved the loss of that nationality.

A genuinely Soviet writer, a member of the supreme parliamentary body of the U.S.S.R. and a colonel of the Red Army, one who had several times forfeited her rights to Polish nationality and who felt at home in the Soviet Union, had become head of the Union of Polish Patriots.

---

* Helen Usiyevich describes him as a " mason-worker, one of the most prominent worker leaders in Cracow " (p. 13). In any case, during his stay in Lvov, Bogatko disappeared in mysterious circumstances.

Besides Wanda Wasilewska, there were nine members of the Presidium of the Union, the highest executive and administrative organ of the " Patriots." Their signatures are given, *inter alia*, under a resolution adopted by the Union on June 23rd, 1944. We hope the reader will excuse us for dwelling a little on the personal history of those members, which seems to us to merit attention.

Of *Berling* we shall speak later on.

Dr. Boleslaw Drobner was struck off the members' list of the Polish Socialist Party in 1936 after eight years' membership. In 1940, he was deported by the Soviet authorites to the U.S.S.R. as unreliable, apparently on account of his constant vacillation between Socialism and Communism. Released from detention by virtue of the Polish-Soviet Agreement, Drobner applied for the post of " local trustee " to the Polish Embassy's organisation of welfare centres. However, he was not accepted.

Andrzej Witos is a half-brother of the great Polish Peasant leader, Wincenty Witos. Once a member of the Peasant Party, though never on any of its governing committees, A. Witos was expelled from that Party in 1928, and went over to the service of the so-called Colonels' regime.

Dr. Stefan Jędrychowski, a well-known Communist from Vilno, voluntarily acquired Soviet nationality, joined the All-Union Communist Party and became a deputy to the Supreme Soviet of the U.S.S.R. After the outbreak of the Nazi-Soviet war Jędrychowski was one of the first to leave Vilno for the safety of the distant Kuybyshev region where he found himself already in the first half of July, 1941. To his dismay, he was given the job of an agricultural worker on a sovkhose (State farm) called Privolzhye, where " I was offered"—as he wrote in a letter to a friend—" the job of a helper doing auxiliary agricultural work. The maximum I can earn is five roubles a day. This is only sufficient for food, provided that I eat only twice a day—soup, groats, and bread. After I have worn out my clothes—and I took only what I wore at the time of the evacuation—which, by the way, are not suitable for agricultural work, I shall find myself in an impossible situation." Therefore, pointing out that the " Fascists would be expelled from our Socialist father-land " before winter came, Jedrychowski asked his friend to find a more remunerative job for him. His request seems to have been given favourable consideration, since, some time after, Jędrychowski was appointed to the post of deputy head of the Polish section of the Tass Agency.

General Aleksander Zawadzki was born in Warsaw, but in 1915, as a youth, he came with his family to Russia. He took part in the Bolshevik Revolution, fighting in 1920 in the Polish-Soviet war within the ranks of the Red Army. In 1935, Zawadzki, then a colonel of the frontier guard forces of the N.K.V.D., controlled a sector of the Soviet Manchurian frontier. A year later, as result of a personal conflict with one of his superiors, Zawadzki was expelled from the All-Union Communist Party. Some time later, he was arrested, degraded and sentenced to 10 years imprisonment on a charge of alleged collaboration with foreign intelligence services. In July, 1941, Zawadzki was in the Onega River Reformatory Labour Camp (the Oneglag). After the conclusion of the Polish-Soviet Military Agreement of August 14th, 1941, Zawadzki contrived to obtain his release from the camp. In 1943, he found his way on to the War Council of the Soviet-Polish Corps, which was composed of Berling, Swierczewski and himself. His swift return to the grade of colonel, and his further career, are a good testimony both of his unusual gifts and his usefulness for the Soviet authorities.

Father Franciszek (recte Wilhelm) Kupsz, a Catholic priest from Polesie, Eastern Poland, after being released by partisans from Pinsk Prison, where he had been put by the Nazis in 1942, joined a Soviet guerilla detachment, and, in June, 1943, was taken to Moscow by a Soviet plane to be appointed chaplain to the Kosciuszko Division. In January, 1944, Father Kupsz was already Dean of the Soviet-Polish Corps.

Dr. Stanislaw Skrzeszewski was known in pre-war Cracow, where he was a schoolmaster, for his Communist convictions.

Dr. Emil Sommerstein was in pre-war Poland a deputy to the Seym from the Zionist Party. Arrested in 1939 by the Soviet authorities and deported to the U.S.S.R. he spent three years in prison, from which he was released under the Polish-Soviet Agreement of July 30th, 1941. In 1943, he was forced by the Soviet authorities to accept Soviet nationality, on the ground that he had been domiciled at Lvov, Eastern Poland.

Dr. Jerzy Sztachelski i sa Communist from Vilno. In 1940 he voluntarily acquired Soviet nationality, becoming a member of the All-Union Communist Party.

To sum up, the Presidium of the Union of Polish Patriots consisted on June 23rd, 1944, of : four Soviet nationals (Jędrychowski, Sztachelski, Wasilewska and Zawadzki) and one person who had signed a formula of loyalty to the Soviet Union (Berling), five Communists (Berling, Jędrychowski, Skrzeszewski, Sztachelski, Wasilewska and Zawadzki), one Communist sympathiser (Drobner), who may be assumed to have joined the '' Polish Workers' Party '' as against three non-Communists : Kupsz, Sommerstein and Witos, the first being a simple soul, politically primitive, a provincial parish priest, the second a Zionist and the third an opportunist with Peasant Party family connections.

We think that we are quite justified in concluding that the Presidium of the Union of Polish Patriots, if only on account of its composition, was and is nothing but a convenient tool in the hands of the Soviet Government, and that a majority of the Presidium's members have had only very remote connections with Polish patriotism. '' Union of Polish-Speaking Soviet Patriots '' would be a more suitable name for the organisation.

This is what a disillusioned Polish Communist writer has to say about these patriots: '

" Even those politicians with little information about the problem know that the leaders of the Union of Patriots were not with us even in spirit when, after September, 1939, we continued our struggle against the Nazis. Not only did they *not* fight against the Nazis in the period 1939-41, when the whole of Poland and her Government fought, but they assailed fighting Poland with insults and slander at their meetings and in their press at Vilno, at Lvov and elsewhere. They disparaged the Polish Army in France while their true spiritual fatherland collaborated with Germany and maintained with her very correct relations. Mme. Wasilewska and her group who specialised at the time in assailing the Polish Government, kept silence about Nazi atrocities in Poland, and her associates' only sorrow was how best to conduct a persistent campaign against the heroic struggle then waged by the Polish nation in conditions of conspiracy, or, openly, in the Polish forests. Through Przemysl, where thousands of young Poles were kept in prison for having dared to try to get across the frontier to France to the Polish Army, continuous transports of Russian oil and petrol were sent to the Western Front where the Nazis fought against France and Britain. When Polish soldiers blew up one of these transports near Przemysl, they were not recognised as heroes fighting against Nazi savagery for the freedom of their country, but as ' bandits ' who ' obstructed peaceful collaboration between two great empires, Nazi and Soviet,' as they were named both in Nazi and Soviet communiques of the time.''

In fulfilment of its statute (cf. *Wolna Polska*, of May 16th, 1943, issue No. 11), the Union undertook political, propaganda and welfare activities. Its greatest political step was that of providing the Soviet authorities with a '' Polish '' excuse to form a Soviet-Polish Army in the U.S.S.R. (see next chapter). In the field of propaganda, the Union has carried on activities among Polish deportees and detainees, in which it has been hampered by these Poles' first-hand experience of the Soviet regime, while being helped in every way by the Soviet authorities and by the general hopelessness of the situation of the Poles in the U.S.S.R. As to social welfare, the Union seized with Soviet backing the stocks of food, clothing and medical supplies brought to the Soviet Union by the Polish Embassy, which, despite the difficulties put in its way by distances and inadequate communications, had managed to organise a wide network of distribution centres for Poles throughout the Soviet Union.

Outside the U.S.S.R., the Union of Polish Patriots has tried to set up branches in neutral and allied countries.

When, in July, 1944, the Molotov-Ribbentrop Line had been crossed by the Red Army, and when the " Polish Committee of National Liberation " was set up at Chelm on July 22nd, several members of the Union joined the Committee, while the Union itself was subordinated to the authority of the National Council of the Homeland.

CHAPTER XV

THEIR OWN POLISH ARMY

About three months before the severance of Polish-Soviet relations, *New Horizons* published a letter signed " Tadeusz W." which put forward the idea of forming a Polish army on Soviet soil (issue of January 20th, 1943). The signature was not difficult to decode. The writer of the letter was a certain Tadeusz Wicherkiewicz, a lieutenant of the Polish pre-war Army, taken prisoner by the Soviets in September, 1939, and subsequently educated in the Soviet Communist gospel at the " Villa of Bliss " at Malakhovka. In 1941, after the conclusion of the Polish-Soviet Military Agreement, Wicherkiewicz joined the Polish Army in the U.S.S.R., where, in 1942, he made unsuccessful attempts to spread Communist propaganda among the soldiers. In June, 1942, some time before the evacuation of the Polish Army to the Middle East, Wicherkiewicz applied for transfer to the Red Army.

Following the public initiative taken by the Communist lieutenant, the Union of Polish Patriots adopted a resolution recommending that a Polish army should be formed in the

U.S.S.R. to fight against Nazi Germany shoulder to shoulder with the Red Army. Simultaneously, the Union applied to the Soviet Government for permission to form such an army.

On May 9th, 1943, three days after the Polish Embassy had left Kuybyshev a Tass Agency communique announced that the Soviet Government had acceded to the request of the Union, and had expressed their consent to the formation in the Soviet Union of a Polish infantry division named after the Polish national hero of the eighteenth century, Tadeusz Kosciuszko (commander of a Polish army in 1792 defending the country against an invading Russian army, and leader of a rising against the Russians and the Prussians in 1794).

The conscription was subsequently carried out by Soviet draft boards (the so-called Voyenkomats, i.e., branches of the Commissariat of War). The conscripts were only too conscious of the role reserved for the newly created Polish army. The great majority of them had spent a considerable time in Soviet prisons and compulsory labour camps. That was not all. Since mid-January, 1943, the Soviet authorities had been forcing them to accept Soviet nationality on the ground that they came from Eastern Poland. Attempts to resist had met with threats, abuse, arrest, jail, and—in not a few cases—with refined torture.*

Now they were to be Poles again, to fill up the ranks of a " Polish Army."

No wonder that, with the exception of a handful of Communists, there was no willingness to join, although they had been quite eager to serve in the genuine Polish Army.

---

* An Orthodox priest who was arrested for refusing to accept a Soviet passport and who later managed to escape from prison, made the following statement : " The things happening in the cells are terrible. Russian criminals, incited by the authorities, are beating our prisoners and robbing them of their money, property and food. During our exercises they beat us several times a day. Complaints are of no avail. . . . Many are beaten. They are forcing us to accept Soviet passports by all kinds of cruelty. The governor of the jail ordered our prisoners to leave the benches and sleep on the floor. They threatened to send bandits to bring order among the Poles. The lower officials use all devices and pettifoggery to persuade us to take the passports."

The best testimony of this is provided by the following statements made by those who saw the " voluntary " mobilisation for the " Polish Army " :

" At Rozeyevka," says a Pole, " we met about 2,000 of our countrymen who were being transported from Siberia to the Kosciuszko Division. They complained that they had not been called up for service in the Polish Army, and that they were now being forced to serve under the command of a Communist gang—so they called the Union of Polish Patriots."

" In June, 1943," says a Pole of Jewish faith, " man-hunts began in the streets first for men, then for women, who were taken to the ' Voyenkomat,' handed over to a recruitment commission, which at once qualified those caught as fit for army service. Cases of rejection on account of bad health were rare. As a rule, the com-mission demanded that the conscript should sign a declaration to the effect that he was a volunteer."

A Polish couple of Jewish faith pointed out the role played by starvation in the recruitment of the " Polish Corps " : " The local Polish population has absolutely no confidence in the Union of Patriots or the Polish Corps, and if anyone either collaborates with the Union or join the Corps, this is due to starvation."

A woman described the mobilisation for the Kosciuszko Division in the Republic of Komi :

" About May 5th, a military medical board worked at Vilgort ; their task was to examine the fitness of all Poles for military service. The examination was super-ficial and nearly everybody was stated to be fit.

" On May 24th, all the conscripts were loaded on board a steamer at Syvtyvkar. The steamer was over-loaded. On board were about 1,000 men from the neighbouring regions. All those mobilised were being transported to the Kosciuszko Division. Near the departing steamer stood crowds of Poles crying aloud and full of despair. On board the steamer it was also all despair. In the last moment, all sang ' God Save Poland ' (a hymn), ' The Oath ' (an anthem) and the

National Anthem, ' Poland hath not yet perished.'   The
Soviet officials themselves were visibly embarrassed.

The command of the new division was entrusted to
Lieutenant-Colonel Zygmunt Berling, of whose conversion to
Stalinism, confirmed by signing a formula of loyalty to the
Soviet Union, we have already spoken.   Some more informa-
tion about Berling may not be out of place here.

After the conclusion of the Polish-Soviet Military Agreement of August 14th, 1941, Berling and his colleagues were
accepted in the Polish Army, although the rumour of their
conversion had already leaked out from Malakhovka.
Officers were needed, and Berling himself had presented his
stay at Malakhovka in a somewhat different light.   However,
events soon proved that the expectation that Berling would
shake off his newly acquired veneer were entirely unfounded.
Appointed chief of staff of the 5th Infantry Division in formation, Berling entered into touch with the N.K.V.D. authorities
and maintained contact with them despite formal prohibition
by his superiors.   This was duly assessed as an act of in-
subordination, and Berling was transferred to the post of
chief of the Krasnovodsk base.   During the evacuation of
the Polish Army, Berling refused to comply with the order to
proceed to the Middle East.   For this act he was subsequently
struck off the officers' list by the Command of the Polish
Army in the Middle East.

On August 10th, 1943, the Tass Agency issued a communique
in which the Soviet Government's assent was announced to
a further '' request by the Union of Polish Patriots '' to
expand the Polish Army in the U.S.S.R. into a Corps.   Berling
was automatically promoted to the rank of Corps Commander.
The Command of the Kosciuszko Division was entrusted to
a Red Army officer of the name of Wojciech Bewziuk,
appointed Major-General on March 13th, 1944.

The second infantry division to be formed with the Soviet-
Polish Corps was named after the creator and leader of the
Polish Legions serving under Napoleon, General Henryk

Dąbrowski : this general also fought against the Russians General Karol Swierczewski became the first commander o the Dąbrowski Division.

Born in Warsaw, Swierczewski left Poland for Russi during the first world war, took part in the Russian Revolutioɪ of November, 1917, and subsequently joined the Red Army where, after graduating from the Soviet Military Academy he reached the rank of general. In that capacity he wa dispatched to Spain to take part in the civil war under th assumed name of General Walter. He was appointeɪ divisional commander on March 18th, 1944.

After the appointment of General Swierczewski to the pos of deputy-commander of the Soviet-Polish Corps, th Dąbrowski Division was taken over by another Soviet-Polisl Red Army officer, Colonel Antoni Siwicki (appointed Major General on March 13th, 1944). Only a short time back, iɪ June, 1943, Siwicki had greeted a congress of the Union o Polish Patriots on behalf of the Soviet-Polish officers servin with the Red Army.

Alongside these two divisions, several other formation were created, of which the Air Force Regiment " Warsaw ' may be mentioned. Command of this regiment was take over by Tadeusz Wicherkiewicz, mentioned at the beginnin of this chapter, now a major, who in the meantime had beeɪ struck off the officers' list of the Polish Army.

After the Red Army's entry into Poland in 1944, ye another two divisions were formed. The third was named th Traugutt Division (after Romuald Traugutt, head of th secret Polish Government set up during the 1863 rising agains Russia),and the fourth the Kilinski Division (after Jan Kilinski a Warsaw shoemaker, leader of the Warsaw rising against th Russians in 1794). The Red Army Lieutenant-Colone Stanislaw Galicki (of Polish descent ?) of Soviet nationality was charged with the command of the Third Division. Oɪ March 18th, 1944, Galicki became Major-General.

As we see from the above survey, most of the higher posts in the Soviet-Polish Army were given to Red Army officers, some of them of Polish descent, of whose political reliability the appropriate Soviet authorities had apparently no doubts whatsoever, their views having been shaped in the hard Soviet mould. Except for some scanty knowledge of Polish, they had no ties with the country of their ancestors or of their youth.

Of the ten generals of Berling's Army serving there in the spring of 1944, nine, that is, all except Berling himself, were Soviet men of the kind described above.*

The picture presented by the rest of the officers' corps was slightly different. It is estimated that these were, after the completion of the second (Dąbrowski) Division, 45 per cent. Poles, not all of them entitled to Polish nationality, while the rest were non-Poles, most of them—certainly 30 per cent. Russians, Soviet nationals. Later, in a statement dated January 2nd, 1945, General Rola Zymierski said : " . . . to form a new Polish Army and rebuild the armed strength of the nation, we appealed to the U.S.S.R. for help. Our powerful and friendly ally gave us many officers of Polish and others of Russian nationality." " . . . we now have over 30,000 officers, the overwhelming majority of whom are Polish."

This Soviet-officered Army, subjected to the Soviet High Command, not only operationally but also in all other respects, hardly deserved the name of a Polish army at all. It was a Soviet-Polish Army. The use of the names of national

---

* At first, the Soviet military authorities did not seem able to make a proper distinction between the Red Army and the " Polish " Army. *Izvestia*, of March 14th, 1944, published a decree of the Council of People's Commissars of the U.S.S.R. by which a number of Red Army officers were promoted to higher ranks. The decree comprised, i.e., the names of Berling, Bewziuk and Siwicki. This characteristic slip was rectified in the next issue of *Izvestia* where a new decree was published in which the same officers were granted the rank of General as officers of " the Polish Military Corps in the U.S.S.R." at the request of the Union of Polish Patriots and after successfully completing combat studies."

heroes who had fought *against* Russian oppression in the eighteenth and nineteenth centuries was only one more shameless attempt to delude public opinion.

The political education of the soldier is the subject of special attention. Its aim is the fundamental transformation of the soldier's soul, by arousing new feelings of sympathy and hatred to replace those developed in his youth by family, school and contemporaries. Later, the Lublin Committee will undertake the same task for the whole nation. Only after going through intensive schooling of this type, as the instructors maintain, will the army become an effective political weapon in the hands of the new " Polish Government."

To fulfil this task, a Board of Political Education was set up at the very outset, attached to the High Command : the head of this Board became deputy C.-in-C. and this was intended to stress the great importance attached to such education.

At first, the post was taken by General Swierczewski-Walter, former commander of international formations in Spain, who ranks amongst the most trusted Soviet Generals. However, after some time, Swierczewski was replaced by General Zawadzki, who, as a former high officer of the N.K.V.D. was politically more experienced.

Zawadzki did not disappoint the confidence of his superiors. Soon, at the motion of the Presidium of the Union of Polish Patriots, he was advanced to the rank of Major-General by a decree of the Council of People's Commissars of the U.S.S.R. The Presidium stated at the time that " the apparatus of political education had done tremendous work resulting in the compactness, deep patriotism and genuine democratic spirit in the Polish Army in the U.S.S.R." (cf. *Wolna Polska*, issue of May 16th, 1944). This was the merit of our N.K.V.D. dignitary : " The advancement of Colonel Zawadzki to the rank of General is proof of Soviet recognition for his work in the field of education " (broadcast of the Union of Polish Patriots, May 21st, 1944).

Among Zawadzki's staff we find the foremost stars of Lublin : Captain Jędrychowski, the Vilno Communist, now delegate of the Committee in Paris, Lieutenant-Colonel Cholyniak, not long before a lieutenant of the Red Army, Colonel Ochab, now Minister of the Interior of the " Provisional Government," and about 100 Soviet political education experts from respective Soviet political institutions, carefully concealing themselves under various pseudonyms.

In the army itself, the political education officers and N.C.O.'s form a special omni-present service. In strict accordance with the Soviet system, established after the abolishment of so-called " political commissars," they fill the posts of deputy-commanders. They control and direct the life of the army according to instructions received from the Board of Political Education.

What are the main ideas that this specific organisation of political propaganda tries to inculcate in the minds of the soldiers ?

As stated by the *New York Times* Lublin correspondent, William Lawrence, its paramount task is to convince the soldiers that the legal Polish Government does not represent anyone except a reactionary Fascist clique. " This new army is being taught that the London Government did not want to wage war actively with the Germans and that its agents preferred co-operation with the Nazis to collaboration with the Soviet Union." This educational effort is probably one of the most important features of the new Polish Army, and is undoubtedly an important factor in the mobilisation of new and ardent support for the Lublin regime " (a broadcast from Lublin on January 9th, 1945).

On the positive side, the soldiers are being convinced that they owe the Soviet Union gratitude for the modern weapons and equipment such as the Polish Army of 1939 could never boast of. The fact is passed over in silence that this equip.

ment comes from the American Lend-Lease Agreement, as noted by foreign correspondents during a military parade at Lublin in January this year.

The cult of the Red Army is being fostered by the erection of numerous monuments of gratitude in Polish cities and towns. More concrete political ideas are being spread on various festive occasions such as the anniversary of Lenin's death, the anniversary of the Bolshevik Revolution and Stalin's birthday.

The propaganda line of hatred towards the Polish Home Army is carried on incessantly by means of broadcast talks, military papers and at political discussion groups. Much emphasis is laid upon the privileges which the soldiers are likely to enjoy on territories taken away from Germany, up to the Oder and the Neisse.

The political educationalists are feared by the soldiers who understand only too well that the least incautious word may bring about disastrous consequences. However, as they are omni-present, it is not easy to avoid their control.

The authorities must have been satisfied with their work, and, on January 2nd, 1945, General Zymierski devoted them considerable space in his speech broadcast on the Lublin Radio :

> '' The corps of political education officers established by the Union of Patriots showed itself equal to its task. These officers, imbued with the ideology which inspires the Polish community today, have become the soldiers' real spiritual leaders. ''

Given these conditions it is difficult to assess what are the results achieved. According to a Polish-American Communist, Oscar Lange, who has visited the Polish Army Corps in the U.S.S.R. the soldiers' radicalism goes further than that of their political leaders. However, they are against the Kolkhose (collective farm) system, which, let us add, is not fully contrary to the *present* line adopted by the Lublin Committee. The problem of Eastern Poland is in Lange's opinion

delicate. The soldiers persistently refuse to accept the view
that Vilno and Lvov are not Polish. For the most part, they
hail from these regions. According to another testimony,
the majority of the soldiers have successfully withstood the
propaganda of their masters, and this was revealed when
they reached Poland. Friendliness towards the Home Army
of the " hated " Polish Government is very marked. It is
also known that many Soviet-Polish Army soldiers did not
refrain from openly demanding that assistance should be
given to Warsaw during the tragic rising of the autumn of
1944. These facts and many others show that those forced
to serve under Soviet officers and subjected to intensive
propaganda by Soviet experts are fundamentally the same
Poles as their brothers in Scotland, Italy or Holland.

CHAPTER XVI

A SHAM PARTY SYSTEM

We have already dealt with the reconstitution of the Communist Party of Poland under the camouflage name of " The
Polish Workers' Party."

However, the restriction to the proletariat of the cities and
towns implied by the Party's name did not facilitate activities
on a larger social scale. Consequently, a sham party system
had to be created, likely to attract followers from wider circles
of the population. These " parties " or " organisations "
were to be useful also inasmuch as they were to be presented
to the Polish people and to the outside world as allegedly
independent and separate political—or military—bodies.
Thus, so the leaders of the " Workers' Party " hoped—they
would constitute a system likely to offset the democratic party
system centering round the Polish Government.

These " parties " made their appearance some time during
the latter half of 1943, when the organisation of the mother-
party had been judged complete, and when the Red Army's
re-entry into Poland was near.

Among the ramifications of the " Polish Workers' Party " there appeared in 1943 a writers' group, a co-operatists' group, a non-manual workers' group, an artisans' group and an " underground trades unions' movement "—all mentioned in *Wolna Polska*, issue of May 27th, 1944, No. 19, as represented on the so-called " National Council of the Homeland," of which we speak later.

The wide popularity of the Polish Socialist Party led to the setting up of one more " party," termed the " Polish Workers' Socialist Party." The similarity in name to the Polish Socialist Party, a ruse so often used by the Communists, was intended to mislead the proletariat of Polish cities and towns. Later on, in September, 1944, even the addition " Workers' " was dropped, so as to achieve complete identity with the popular party.

In order to attract Poles with more nationalist leanings, a " Committee of National Initiative " was invented (cf. the quoted issue of *Wolna Polska*), the corresponding word for " national " being " narodowy," a word less suggestive of Statehood than of nationalism. Later on, most probably on account of too glaring ideological incompatibility with Communism, the Committee was quietly dropped into oblivion. A group of " Non-party Democrats " was founded with an eye to the Polish democratic intelligentsia. At a later stage, in September, 1944, the group evolved into a fully-fledged " Polish Democratic Party." A war-time convert to Sovietism, Rzymowski, then assumed its leadership.

The issue of *Wolna Polska* already quoted also mentions " the opposition group of the Peasant Party." This was meant to serve to recruit a following among the Polish peasants. In 1943, the " Polish Workers' Party " was still wary enough not to hide under the shield of the Peasant Party, thus acknowledging the real state of affairs, namely, that the peasants were backing the Polish Government ; in September, 1944, however, the Polish Communists had become so emboldened as to drop the designation " opposi-

tion '' altogether. The development was similar to that of
the '' Polish Workers' Socialist Party '' and to the transformation of the group of Democrats into the ''Democratic
Party,'' all during the same period.

Only one racial '' party '' was set up, styled the '' Jewish
Workers' Party.'' This is easily explained. One year later,
in September, 1944, the Polish Committee of National Liberation concluded agreements with the Byelorussian, '' Lithuanian '' and Ukrainian S.S.R., in virtue of which all Byelorussians, Lithuanians and Ukrainians living to the west of the
so-called Curzon Line were to be evacuated to the territories
east of that Line, so as to deprive Committee Poland of all
non-Poles except the Jews. The leaders of the '' Workers'
Party '' must have been advised of this plan as early as 1943,
and they logically decided that no Byelorussian or Ukrainian
sections of the Communist Party of Poland were necessary.
The Jews were to be left where they were living, or perhaps
one would rather say, where they had survived. This ac-
counted for the establishment of the '' Jewish Workers'
Party.'' The newly created ramification of the Communist
Party of Poland was the more necessary as the Jewish proletariat of the towns, remnants of which had managed to
survive Nazi massacres, had been organised by the Jewish
Socialist Party Bund, a member of the Second International,
The Bund, which, alongside the Polish Socialist Party, aimed
at the emancipation of the masses of the Jewish workers
through Socialism within the framework of Polish national
independence, was thoroughly disliked by the Soviets. In
1939, many of its leaders had been imprisoned in Eastern
Poland.

'' The People's Guard '' mentioned in the issue of *Wolna
Polska* quoted above, was, until its place was taken in Poland
by the Soviet-Polish Army, the '' Polish Workers' Party ''
combat organisation, whereas the '' People's Militia '' was
and is the party's political police, today constituting the

mainstay of the N.K.V.D. in Soviet-controlled Polish territory.

The Fighting Youth Association ('' Związek Walki Młodych), is the '' Polish Workers' Party '' youth branch.

In their endeavour to create the pretence of wide popular support, the '' Polish Workers' Party '' did not hesitate to use the names of military organisations owing allegiance to the Polish Government. Thus, they claimed to have won over certain detachments of the Home Army. The procedure was not dissimilar from that adopted in the case of political parties.

The purpose behind the setting up of the above-mentioned ramifications of the Communist Party of Poland masquerading under the name of the '' Polish Workers' Party '' was not only the creation of a sham party system for propaganda abroad. The main purpose of the sham system was to lure as many Poles as possible into the Communist sphere of influence, and thus to collect some ramshackle support for the social and national fabric planned for Poland by the Party. Nevertheless, even under Committee rule in the latter half of 1944, the Polish people have managed to keep aloof from the allegedly independent organisations created and dominated by the '' Polish Workers' Party,'' and no leader of any standing with the people has ever joined any of the '' parties.''

CHAPTER XVII

THE COMMUNIST PARTY AS PARLIAMENT

The Polish Workers' Party, in its quest for power, conceived the idea of transforming itself into a body destined to play the part of a representative Polish parliamentary body. This body was formed secretly in Warsaw on January 1st, 1944, i.e., a few days before the Red Army crossed the Polish-Soviet frontier near Sarny, Volhynia, on January 4th, 1944.

The coincidence in date is easily explained. The Red Army's re-entry into Poland was bound to bring the issue of Polish-Soviet relations before the world again, and therefore, the Soviet leaders had judged it opportune to provide themselves in time with a " Polish parliament " of their own, which would endorse their policy towards Poland.

The name chosen was that of " National Council of the Homeland," an obvious copy of the names of the two already existing parliamentary substitutes connected with the . Polish Government :   the National Council, whose first session was held in Paris on January 23rd, 1940, and the Council of National Unity, formerly the Political Representation of the Homeland, set up in Underground Poland in the winter of 1939-40.

As usual, much effort was spent on creating a pretence that the new body had wide popular support and that its creation was the result of the political dynamism of the Polish masses. The following " parties " and " groups " were declared to have taken part in the setting up of th' Council :   the Polish Workers' Party, the Polish Workers' Socialist Party, the Peasant Party, opposition group, the Committee of National Initiative, a Group of Non-Party Democrats, the Underground Trades Union Movement, the Fighting Youth Association, a Group of Polish Writers, a Group of Co-operatists, a Group of Artisans'. Representatives, and representatives of the People's Guard, of the People's Militia, of the Peasants' Batalions, and of the Regional Formations of the Home Army (cf. *Wolna Polska*, issue of May 24th, 1944, No. 19). We have already dealt with this agglomeration of names and no further comment seems necessary.

As to the mighty surge of political dynamism which was implied to have been at the source of the National Council of the Homeland, information was given in *Wolna Polska*, issue of February 8th, 1944, No. 5, to the effect that " the

Council was elected by the voivodship*, the district and the local councils, which in their turn had been elected by patriotic organisations. Thus, the Council was alleged to have evolved from a wide network of lesser councils. However, it soon appeared that no " lesser " councils had existed before the creation of the National Council of the Homeland.

From the same *Wolna Polska* issue of July 24th, 1944, No. 27, we derive the information that the voivodship council of such an important Polish Region as Upper Silesia was created only at the beginning of May, 1944, i.e., over four months after the National Council of the Homeland was first founded. A leaflet signed by the Voivodship council of the Lublin Province dated March 8th, 1944, contains the information that this council was formed " in accordance with the requirements of the provisional statute of national councils," which statute, let us add, had been adopted at the first session of the National Council of the Homeland on January 1st, 1944. We may therefore, safely discard the pretence that the National Council of the Homeland was built up on a solid background of lesser councils and conclude that, in actual fact, the structure was extended from above. This is almost literally stated in the *Wolna Polska* for May 24th, 1944, issue No. 19 : " During its several months' activity, the National Council of the Homeland has already managed to set up throughout the country a network of its own territorial organisations (communal, district, town and voivodship) "—from a communique of the Union of Polish Patriots.

Needless to say, the " territorial organisations," i.e., the communal, district, town and voivodship councils, were none other than the " Polish Workers' Party " in a new incarnation, possibly with a few "" amenables " to provide the necessary camouflage.

If it is true that the person of the chairman of an organisation gives the best measure for assessing the real character of

---

* The voivodship is the highest administrative territorial unit in Poland.

that organisation, we ought to devote a little attention to M. Eugeniusz Boleslaw Bierut, chairman of the National Council of the Homeland.

His real name is not known for certain, Bierut being a party pseudonym. During the first world war, he went to Russia, whence he came back to Poland in December, 1923, after a three-year schooling in Moscow in Komintern work. During 1923-25, Bierut was one of the underground leaders of the Communist Party of Poland. Involved in the affair of the escape from justice of another Komintern agent, Leszczynski, Bierut, for whom search was being made, had to escape from Poland. He was first in Vienna, and later in Prague, working in both places for the secret Komintern bureau for South-Eastern Europe, as head of the Polish section. In 1932, his work again took him to Poland. However, he soon found himself arrested and sentenced to seven years imprisonment. His Soviet nationality was of assistance to him here, for, a year later, Bierut was included in an exchange of political prisoners with the U.S.S.R. In 1933-4, he went through a special Komintern course at Leningrad. 1935 and 1936 saw him in Moscow. In 1936, Bierut was entrusted with the post of head of the Polish section of the foreign department of the O.G.P.U. (now known as the N.K.V.D.).

His third trip to Poland dates from a little before the present war. The Soviet occupation found him in Lvov. He spent the period 1939-41 there, directing N.K.V.D. measures against " unreliable " Poles, Ukrainians and Jews. When the Nazis approached Lvov in the course of their campaign against the U.S.S.R., Bierut retreated to Moscow. Within a few months, however, he found himself back on Polish territory, where he was dropped by parachute. He undertook to organise and lead the newly established " Polish Workers' Party " (cf. *The Polish Daily*, January 9th, 1945).

With the exception of Mr. Bierut, whose politics, as we can see, have been clearly defined, the names of the other 29 of the Council's members during 1944 have never been given in public jointly. Only after laborious digging in the various sources of information available in this country can we establish the names of 13 members, the other 16 we have to leave to their anonymity.

We are in a position to give a little information on some 13 known members of the Council :

Edward Boleslaw Osubka-Morawski, vice-chairman of the Council, was a minor official in a Socialist Flats Co-operative in Warsaw. During the war, he joined the Polish Workers' Party, and subsequently worked for it within the group called the Polish Socialist Workers' Party.

Jan Czechowski was alleged by the '' Soviet Monitor,'' No. 5155, to have been one of the chief promoters of the Polish Peasant Movement, and as such to have become in 1916 one of the founders of the peasant party of '' Libera-tion '' ('' Wyzwolenie ''), later on merged in a joint Peasant Party. The same sources maintain that Czechowski was one of the founders of the Polish Left-Wing People's Government formed in 1918 at Lublin, and that, in 1925, he was elected to the Seym as a candidate of the '' Liberation '' Party. In actual fact, Czechowski's name is entirely unknown to persons with a thorough knowledge of Polish internal politics in 1916-25.

Jan Stefan Haneman was a bank clerk at Lodz before the war, and a member of an Atheist organisation with marked Communist sympathies. After the secret arrival of Bierut in Poland during the winter of 1941-42, Haneman became his liaison-agent and travelled throughout Poland distributing Communist Party literature to the various party cells.

Stanislaw Agroszewski acted as Komintern agent in Poland in the period 1936-38. His Party pseudonym is Kotek. Soviet sources style him as a member of the Peasant Party. According to our information he was one of the Political Bureau of the '' Polish Workers' Party '' and as such was entrusted with the supervision of the activities of the Party towns' and cities' groups.

Kazimierz Hardy is one of the organisers of the " Polish Workers' Party." His real name is not known, *Hardy* being a party pseudonym.

Szymon Zolna was before the war a teacher at a teachers' training college in Kielce. In 1942/3 he acted as a member of the Political Bureau of the " Polish Workers' Party."

General Michal Rola-Zymierski (recte Lyzwinski) : Collaborated in the organisation of the Sharpshooters' Commands in former Austrian Poland in 1911/14. He joined the Polish Legions, a military formation fighting for Polish independence during the first World War. After completing studies at the Ecole Superieure de Guerre, Paris, Zymierski was appointed General in 1924. In 1926 he was sentenced to several years' imprisonment on a charge of graft and cashiered. Released after serving part of the sentence, Zymierski settled in Paris and got into touch with purveyors of armaments to Spain. Some time before the war, Zymierski returned to Poland, and stayed in Warsaw and in Lvov under the Nazi occupation. In November, 1943, already then a member of the " Polish Workers' Party," Zymierski emerged in Volhynia with a group of Communist-led guerrillas.

According to Mr. Bierut (cf. his speech delivered at a Congress of Chairmen of National Councils held on September 21st-23rd, 1944), the Council's legal basis of existence is the Polish democratic constitution of 1921. Mr. Bierut also alleges that the Council has all the prerogatives of the Polish Seym (the Lower Chamber) and Senate (the Upper Chamber). However, even the most careful analysis of the 1921 constitution fails to reveal articles thereof which might be used in support of Mr. Bierut's assertions, and he has given proof of his tactical sagacity in avoiding any reference to specific stipulations of the 1921 constitution.

In the middle of May, 1944, the delegation of the National Council of the Homeland, with Mr. Osubka-Morawski at its head, made a trip to Moscow, in order to get in touch with the Soviet leaders and the Union of Patriots. Thence the members of the delegation came back to Poland with the Russian armies in the latter half of July, 1944, and an administrative emanation of the " Polish Workers' Party," the Committee of Liberation was started.

PART III

CHAPTER XVIII

THE LUBLIN COMMITTEE SETTLES IN POLAND

The Moscow visit of the Council of the Homeland had been well-timed. Two months later, the Red Army crossed the Bug, and, on June 22nd, 1944, captured Chełm (Kholm), a town in Central Poland, not far from the Molotov-Ribbentrop Partition Line of 1939. In the wake of the Red Army, there entered Chełm on the same day a body composed of members drawn from the National Council of the Homeland and the Union of Polish Patriots, and apparently agreed upon during the visit to the Kremlin in May.—This body styled it'elf the " Polish Committee of National Liberation," and, on the day of Chełm's capture—laudable alacrity—issued a long-winded manifesto to the Polish nation.

The Committee was formally set up by a decree of the National Council of the Homeland, dated, for obvious reasons, Warsaw, 21st July, 1944, as a " provisional executive authority to lead the nation's struggle for liberation, and to secure its independence and the re-establishment of the Polish State." Another decree of the Council declared that the Council " as the sole representative of the nation entitled to lead and co-ordinate all activities directed towards the liberation of Poland . . . assumed supreme authority over the Union of Polish Patriots in the U.S.S.R. and the Polish Army in the U.S.S.R. (i.e., the Soviet-Polish Army dealt with earlier in this work) which is under its authority."

Edward Bolesław Osubka-Morawski assumed the chairmanship of the Committee. We know him already. There were two vice-chairmen : Wanda Wailewsska and Andrzej Witos, both of whom were delegated from the Presidium of the Union of Patriots.

In accordance with the task entrusted to it, the Committee was composed of 13 administrative departments. Osubka-

Morawski was at the head of the Department of Foreign Affairs. Andrzej Witos became Head of the Department of Agriculture. His appointment was calculated to gain peasant support for the Committee. The calculation was not bad, in view of the fact that his elder half-brother, Wincenty, had been the approved leader of Polish peasantry. As such, Wincenty Witos had become Premier of Poland in 1920, when the country was threatened by Bolshevik aggression. During a later period Wincenty Witos was one of the most prominent supporters of agrarian reform, and a generally recognised leader of the peasant's struggle for educational and cultural emancipation. The magic influence of the name was decidedly something to make full use of, and this was why —the insignificant little brother was appointed vice-chairman and member of the Committee.

The Department of National Defence was entrusted to General Rola-Zymierski, of whom we spoke in the previous chapter. Berling became his deputy. The subordination of Berling to Zymierski was somewhat unexpected. To our knowledge, Zymierski had not had the advantage of having gone through a course like the one by means of which Berling and his brother officers had been selected at Malakhovka in the " Villa of Bliss.'' The prevailing factor in the inner counsels of the Committee's preceptors was probably that, unlike Berling, Zymierski had been in Poland all through the Nazi occupation, and must have acquired an intimate know-ledge of the prevailing conditions there from his own experi-ence.

The Departments of Public Administration, National Economy and Finance, and of Justice were respectively en-trusted to Stanisław Kotek-Agroszewski, Jan Stefan Haneman and Jan Czechowski, of whom we spoke in the preceding chapter.

Stanisław Radkiewicz, a member of the Polish Workers' Party, was appointed head of the Department of Public Security.

Dr. Bolesław Drobner, formerly a member of the Presidium of the Union of Patriots. was entrusted with the post of Head of the Department of I abour. Social Welfare and Public Health.

Engineer Jan Michał Grubecki was appointed Head of the Department of Communications, Posts and Telegraphs. He had been Head of the Department of Social Welfare of the Union of Polish Patriots. Up to then he had been almost entirely unknown among Poles, and it was only after protracted enquiries that we were able to discover that during his studies at the Higher Engineering School of Lvov he had displayed Right-Wing views.

Dr. Emil Sommerstein, the Zionist of the Union of Patriots, became Head of the Department of War Reparations.

Dr. Stanisław Skrzeszowski, of the Presidium of the " Patriots " was entrusted with the Department of Education.

Wincenty Rzymowski became Head of the Department of Culture and Arts.

Dr. Stefan Jędrychowski was entrusted with the Department of Propaganda and Information.

To sum up, the Lublin Committee, or the " Polish Workers' Party," as an executive governmental body, comprised eight Communists (Morawski. Wasilewska, Zymierski, Agroszewski, Haneman, Radkiewicz. Skrzeszewski, and Jędrychowski), one Communist sympathiser (Drobner) with the usual addition of four amenable non-Communists to provide the necessary camouflage (Andrzej Witos, Grubecki, Sommerstein and Rzymowski)—and not likely to exert any influence. All the key posts (chairman, one vice-chairman, public administration, public security, justice, national economy and finance and propaganda) were in Communist hands.

CHAPTER XIX

THE COMMITTEE'S MANIFESTO

What was the political programme of the Committee ?

In the Chelm manifesto of July 22nd, 1944, the Committee announced their desire to wage war " side by side with the Red Army, until the Polish flag flies . . . in Berlin."

In this their stand differed from that taken by the Polish Government only inasmuch as the latter had been conducting the Polish nation's struggle against Germany since 1939. That the 75,000 Polish Army raised in the U.S.S.R. in the period 1941-2 could not take part in the war side by side with the Red Army was not the fault of the Polish Government, but was due to the settled policy of the Soviet leaders (this army later fought in Italy). Undeterred by this experience, the Polish Government, in their endeavour to reach an honourable understanding with the U.S.S.R., had instructed their Home Army as early as October, 1943, to help the Red Army in campaigning through Poland by carrying out local actions against the Nazis whenever the Red Army was approaching (cf. *The Times*, September 1st, 1944). By July 22nd, 1944, the date of the manifesto, considerable help had been rendered to the Red Army by the Home Army, including the participation in the capture of Vilno (July 13th) and Lvov (July 26th), where—let us remark—the Red Army could not boast of any support from either Lithuanian or Ukrainian quarters. Nazi-controlled railway lines in Poland leading to the Eastern Front had been constantly sabotaged all the time by the same Home Army, so that considerable quantities of supplies and reinforcements had been prevented from reaching the front.

Nevertheless, the Committee felt entitled to express its dissatisfaction with the Polish Government. The manifesto declared : " The emigré Government in London and its agency in Poland is an illegal and self-styled authority, based on the illegal Fascist Constitution of April, 1935. That

easily understandable in a body representing an infinitesimal minority of the nation, and aspiring to establish a one-party dictatorship.

The attack on the 1935 Constitution leaves us unmoved. However, we may say that both the Polish constitutions, that of 1921 and that of 1935, had their good and bad points, and that when really free conditions are re-established in Poland, the Polish people, wiser by so much experience, acquired both before and during the war, will elect worthy representatives to formulate a new one. For the time being, the constitution at present in force must be respected, for otherwise the Polish State would drift into legal chaos and uncertainty.

The Communist Committee's attachment for the " bourgeois-democratic " 1921 constitution has a different explanation. If the Party yearns for it and hysterically deprecates the constitution of 1935, it is not out of love for bourgeois democracy, as they could not with justice be suspected of any such indecency.* The reasons are twofold. First, the Committee men wish to abolish the legal basis of the Polish Government—second, the 1921 constitution provides for Presidential power to be transferred in certain circumstances to the Speaker of the Seym. As the reader remembers, the National Council of the Homeland previously assumed the position of the Polish Parliament. Once having become a " Parliament," its Speaker, Mr. Bierut, would, as the alleged chairman of a duly elected Seym, rise to the position of Poland's acting President.

To continue the examination of the Chełm Manifesto, the allegation that the Polish Government " has hampered the struggle against the Hitlerite invaders " is now an old-fashioned one both in Lublin and Soviet propaganda. The tragic Warsaw rising of August 1st — October 2nd, 1944, of

---

* To justify Lithuania's annexation in 1940, the 1938 Lithuanian " Fascist " constitution owing to which the so-called " People's Government " came into being—had been good enough for the Lithuanian Communists.

which the whole world has heard despite many efforts to the contrary, has struck this preposterous weapon out of the hands of Poland's enemies. However, since forgetfulness is the common weakness of all nations, let us recall a few episodes of this war which were not entirely unconnected with the work of the Polish Government.

In May, 1940, Polish forces under the orders of the Polish Government took part in the Norway expedition. Two Polish divisions raised on French soil by the same Government helped the French to fight the Nazis in May-June of the same year. Polish airmen shot down 12 per cent. of Nazi aircraft in aerial combat over this country in September, 1940, i.e., during the Battle of Britain. A Polish Brigade took part, in 1941, in the Africa fighting (the defence of Tobruk). Again the Polish Air Force carried out many operations alongside the R.A.F., and the Polish Navy and Merchant Marine played their part at the side of their British sister-services. Since 1943, the Polish Army evacuated from the U.S.S.R. in 1942 has been fighting in Italy. Then again, since D-day, Polish forces have been fighting in France, Belgium and Holland side by side with their British, Canadian, American and French comrades-in-arms. Polish intelligence services were the first to furnish the British authorities with timely evidence and information concerning Germany's secret weapons, Polish airmen had a considerable share in the number of flying-bombs shot down by aircraft (cf. *The Polish Daily*, September 9th, 1944; out of 1,900 bombs shot down by fighters, 223 were shot down by Poles.)

In Poland itself, the struggle has never been given up, and this not since 1941, the year of the Nazi attack on the U.S.S.R., but since 1939. It took the form of sabotaging the Nazi war effort, hindering communications, killing off German hangmen and of numerous encounters with S.S. and Reichs-

---

* Cf. p. 31, " First to Fight "—Peter Jordan, published London, 1944 : " The ratio of Polish victories to those of the whole R.A.F. in September, 1940, was 1 : 7.2."

wehr detachments. All that was the result of combined efforts of the Polish Underground and the Polish Government.

The charge of " political opportunism " is the more ridiculous, as apart from the struggle carried on against Nazi Germany, the Polish Government has taken an unflinching stand against the steady flow of propaganda, slander and abuse emanating since 1942 from the East, and still further augmented after the severance by the Soviet Government of diplomatic relations on April 25th, 1943.

Let us now proceed with the further examination of the Committee's Manifesto.

The Committee called upon the Polish nation to intensify the struggle against the Nazis : "Take up arms. Strike the Germans wherever you meet them. Attack their transport. Obey the mobilisation decreed in liberated territory and join the ranks of the Polish Army. . . ."

One remark at least might be made in connection with this passage. It concerns the " Polish Army " of the Manifesto. A decree of the Council of the Homeland, dated Warsaw, July 21st, 1944, had stipulated a union of the " People's Army," the combat organisation of the Communist Party of Poland, known also as the " People's Guard," with the Polish Army raised under General Berling, into a joint Polish Army. As we showed earlier, Berling's army rather deserved to be called a " Soviet-Polish Army." The new joint army composed of the Soviet-Polish Army and of the Communist People's Army, could not be termed otherwise. This is confirmed by the appointment of General Aleksander Zawadzki, already known to us, as one of the two deputy-commanders of the joint army.

Territorially, the Manifesto presented the Soviet Government's programme as formulated by the latter during the Polish-Soviet conversations of July-August, 1944, and September, 1944. In the west, the future Poland was to comprise Pomerania and Silesia up to the Oder, and in the north, the inclusion of East Prussia was advocated. In the East,

Poland's frontier was to run along the Curzon Line, differing from the Ribbentrop-Molotov Line chiefly inasmuch as the former gave Poland the region of Białystok and Suwalki.

Further, the Committee announced the setting up of a Citizens' Militia, an organisation only too reminiscent of the People's Militia, the political police organisation of the Communist Party of Poland, and that not only in name, as subsequent events proved. " Fascist organisations "—ran the Manifesto—" will be stamped out with the utmost severity of the law." As the terms " Fascist " (and " anti-Soviet ") are not infrequently used rather loosely by the Communists, the danger arose that any organisation not likely to follow meekly the Communist lead might be " stamped out " by the Committee.

Finally the Manifesto of the Committee promised a " free, strong, independent, sovereign and democratic Poland." Here the Committee's political originality showed itself at its best. Consider the shower of high-sounding adjectives : " free," " strong," " independent," " sovereign," and " democratic "—as against the admirably restrained vocabulary of Marshal Stalin's statement to the *Times* Moscow correspondent, on May 4th, 1943, in which Poland was spoken of as " strong " and " independent."

The Committee ended its mission on December 31st, 1944, i.e., after something more than half a year's rule in part of Poland. We shall later attempt to examine what conditions it had created in that part of Polish national territory which found itself under its sway after its liberation from Nazi tyranny.

CHAPTER XX

THE COMMITTEE AND THE WARSAW RISING

" Strike the Germans wherever you meet them," said the Committee's Manifesto of July 22nd, 1944.

Warsaw, Poland's Capital, had been a " meeting-place " of Poles and Germans for almost five years at the time, so that " wherever you meet them " might well have applied to Warsaw too.

As if to bring this point out, two broadcasts specifically addressed to Warsaw were given from Soviet territory :

> " For Warsaw, which did not yield but fought on, the hour of action has already arrived. The Germans will no doubt try to defend themselves in Warsaw. It is therefore a hundred times more necessary than ever to remember that in the flood of Hitlerite destruction all is lost that is not saved by active effort, that by direct struggle in the streets of Warsaw, in its houses, factories and stores we not only hasten the moment of final liberation, but also save the nation's property and the lives of our brothers " (July 30th, 1944—Moscow, Union of Polish Patriots).

> " People of Warsaw, to arms ! The whole population should gather round the National Council and the Underground Army. Attack the Germans ! Stop the Germans destroying public buildings. Assist the Red Army in crossing the Vistula. Give it information and show it the best fords. The more than a million inhabitants should become an army of a million men fighting for liberation and destroying the German invaders " (July 30th, 1944—the " Kościuszko " station).

The first of these broadcasts, both repeated several times, was given in the name of an organisation of which seven out of ten of the leaders were either vice-chairmen (Wasilewska, Witos) heads of departments of the Committee (Drobner, Jędrychowski, Skrzeszewski, Sommerstein) or deputy heads of departments (Berling). The second was given by a former Komintern station which in its farewell broadcast of August 22nd, 1944, recommended to its listeners the service of the Committee's Broadcasting Station, set up at Lublin on August 10th, 1944.

Consequently we may assume, and we shall not be far wrong, that the Committee has some share of responsibility for the two broadcasts appealing to Warsaw to rise.

On August 1st, 1944, the Red Army approached the outskirts of Warsaw and a rising broke out in the capital against
the Nazis. It was led by the Home Army, the military
organisation connected with the legal Polish Government.
About 25,000 men, i.e., as many as could dispose of any kind
of arms, rose up against the Germans in open combat, with a
view to liberating the Capital and helping the Red Army to
cross the Vistula at Warsaw. When this had happened, the
Red Army suddenly halted before Warsaw, and, after initial
successes gained by the insurgents, the Nazis were free to
massacre the people and devastate the city.

To make things entirely clear, the order for the rising had
been given by the Home Army Commander, General Bor,
who acted in accordance with general instructions sent him
by the Polish Government in October, 1943 (cf. the *Times*,
September 1st, 1944). Nevertheless, in taking the decision,
Bor took into account the Union and Kościuszko broadcasts,
which to him were an expression of the wishes of these two
bodies, undoubtedly—as he rightly assumed—acting on
behalf of the Red Army Command.

On August 17th, the Committee's Broadcasting station in
Lublin declared its solidarity with the Warsaw rising :

   " Our camp, the camp of fighting democracy, has
   always welcomed any sign of fighting against the German
   invader. We have always called you to arms and have
   seen in an active struggle the surest means of saving men
   and national property. We see in the present rising in
   Warsaw a manifestation of the fighting spirit of the
   democratic camp, and the Warsaw fighting is to us as
   sacred as any act of combat against the enemy."

In his Moscow conversations with Marshal Stalin and
Commissar Molotov, the Polish Premier Mikołajczyk was
assured that Warsaw would probably be taken by the Red
Army by August 6th (cf. *The Times*, September 1st, 1944).
General Bor's calculations were similar. However, contrary
to expectations, the insurgents had to continue the rising until
October 2nd, 1944, i.e., during 63 days. Supplies of arma-

ments and food were quickly being exhausted, and the capital badly needed help.

Nevertheless, no assistance was forthcoming from the Committee. Only in mid-September were parts of Berling's forces used for the limited operation of capturing Praga, a suburb of Warsaw situated on the eastern bank of the Vistula (Warsaw lies on its western bank).

Up to that time, not only had the Committee's Air Force Regiment, formed in the U.S.S.R. in 1943,* not gone to the capital's assistance, although its Supreme Commander (General Zymierski) was a Committee member, but that same Commander either acquiesced in or himself carried out the disarming of Home Army detachments trying to get through Committee Poland to Warsaw's defence (cf. *The Times*, October 3rd, 1944).

Although detailed information as to the places in Warsaw where supplies could safely be dropped by parachute had been given as early as August 10th, 12th and 16th, in Bor's dispatches transmitted to Moscow (cf. *The Times*, September 12th, 1944) General Zymierski alleged that prior to the 13th September, he did not know where the supplies ought to be landed (cf. a broadcast in the Soviet European Service of October 1st, 1944). On August 28th, the General had asserted that " it was impracticable to supply arms or troops by air, because most of them would be bound to fall into German hands (cf. *The Times*, August 30th, 1944), as the insurgents held " only isolated buildings " (*Daily Worker*, August 30th, 1944). However, supplies and arms were delivered by the Soviet Air Force in mid-September, when the area held by the insurgents had actually considerably shrunk. They were belated, inadequate both in quantity and quality, dropped mostly without parachute, but come they did.

---

* Its commander was Major Tadeusz Wicherkiewicz, the lieutenant of the " Villa of Bliss " who first made public the plan to form a Soviet-Polish Army.

It may also be noted that the Chairman of the Committee, Osubka-Morawski, declared on September 30th, 1944, at a press conference in Moscow, that the leader of the Warsaw rising, General Bor " was a criminal to the Polish nation for it was he who caused the population to rise prematurely " (cf. Soviet European Service in Polish, October 1st, 1944). Naturally enough, he did not dwell upon the two appeals of the end of July.

The Warsaw rising ended in a great national disaster. Up to 250,000 people lost their lives, this number including about 12,500 men and officers of the Home Army (the· rest became Nazi prisoners of war).

This tragedy might have been averted, or at least mitigated to a great extent if adequate help had been given as General Bor had requested since August 1st (cf. *The Times*, September 12th, 1944). If the Committee did not care for the Home Army (which was an organisation comprising all Polish elements with the exclusion of the Right-wing and Left-wing, i.e., Communist, extremists) and if it was jealous of the attachment and devotion shown to it by the Polish people, they at least should have cared for the people of Warsaw and for the capital itself. Any genuinely Polish authority would have done so. Not the Lublin Committee.

CHAPTER XXI

POPULATIONS SHIFTED

On September 9th, 1944, the Committee concluded in Lublin agreements with the Governments of the Byelorussian and the Ukrainian S.S.R. concerning a mutual transfer of populations (cf. *The Times*, September 15th, 1944). On September 22nd, 1944, the Committee concluded a similar agreement with the Government of the " Lithuanian S.S.R." (Lublin broadcast of September 23rd, 1944).

In passing we may note that the setting up of a " Lithuanian S.S.R." has not been approved yet by any Allied or neutral government in the world, except that of the U.S.S.R. By concluding an agreement with the government of that body, the Committee showed only once more that it is entirely dependent on Soviet instructions.

The transfers provided for by the three Committee's agreements were to be effected from " Committee Poland," i.e., the Polish territory situated to the west of the so-called Curzon Line, to the territories, both Soviet and Soviet-claimed, to the east of the Line.

According to the Polish estimate for August 31st, 1939, the Polish territory east of the Line was the home of 4,304,000 Poles, whereas the territory west of the Line was inhabited by 69,000 Byelorussians, 8,000 Lithuanians and 505,000 Ukranians. Since the agreement between the Committee and Soviet Lithuania provided for a transfer of Poles from pre-war Lithuanian territory also, some 150,000 in number, the number of persons liable to transfer would amount to 4,454,000 on the Polish side and 582,000 on the Byelorussian-Lithuanian-Ukrainian side, all according to an estimate for the day preceding the outbreak of the second world war.

Option for transfer was to be made by December 1st, 1944. The transfer itself was to be effected between December 1st, 1944, and April 1st, 1945, from the " Lithuanian S.S.R."* and vice versa, or between December 1st, 1944, and February 1st, 1945, from the Byelorussian S.S.R. and the Ukrainian S.S.R. and vice versa†, i.e., within four or two months.

The months concerned are winter months. Anybody familiar with the Eastern European winter knows that this is not a time suitable for transfers of population, the more so as the territories involved have been devastated by years of war and occupation, and as there is a shortage of housing, food and clothing, and transport facilities are to say the least inadequate, having regard to the virtual monopoly of transport by the fighting forces.

The territory under Committee control had on August 31st, 1939, a population of about 5,000,000 up to the Soviet offensive of mid-January, 1945. Even enlarged during the latter half of January, 1945, the territory was certainly not capable of an intake of a theoretical number of 4,454,000 Poles during two to four winter and war months. It may be recalled that it took about a year and a half to complete the Greco-Turkish mutual transfer of population, that this transfer covered only about one-ninth of the theoretical number liable to transfer under the Committee agreements, that it was carried out in peace-time under international control and by virtue of a freely negotiated agreement by two internally and internationally recognised Governments††. Nevertheless, the Greco-Turkish transfer was responsible for much human suffering, inevitably connected with any transfer of population on a large scale. (For footnotes see next page).

To stay in Eastern Poland or Lithuania was for the Poles there tantamount to accepting Soviet rule for good. In view of the fact that the proportion of Poles favouring Communism does not exceed 2 per cent. (cf. the pamphlet by the Socialist writer, Adam Ciołkosz and others, '' Democratic Poland answers,'' p. 9, where he states '' According to recent reports

---

* Cf. an article by O. Savich, '' Poles and Lithuanians Solve a National Minorities Problem,'' published *The Soviet War News Weekly*, issue of October 12th, 1944.

† Cf. an article of the Committee's official daily *Rzeczpospolita* broadcast from Lublin on October 30th, 1944, and reporting that the transfer Commission at Przemysl will have completed its work by February 1st, 1945.

†† The Greco-Turk exchange of population was effected under the Lausanne Convention of January 30th, 1923. The task of supervising the execution of the transfer was entrusted to a Mixed Commission consisting of four Greek and four Turkish representatives, and of three members appointed by the Council of the League of Nations from neutral countries. In 1927, the two Governments concerned agreed to reduce the number of their representatives to two each.

The exchange proper was effected during the period October 7th, 1923—March 21st, 1925. During that period, covering about one year and half, 547,003 persons were exchanged. However, in view of the complicated property issues, the Mixed Commission did not end its work until October 19th, 1934 (cf. report communicated to the Council of the League of Nations by the Representative of France, on January 12th, 1935, entitled '' Close of the Work of the Mixed Commission for the Exchange of Greek and Turkish Population.'')

from Poland the followers of Communism in that or any other guise amount to about 2 per cent. of the Polish Underground Movement '') it is safe to assume that at least four million Poles would prefer to leave the homeland of their ancestors and join the main bulk of the nation, could they be assured that the Soviet regime would not be extended to Central and Western Poland, and provided they were given really free choice. This would amount to accepting four million people into an area already containing (up to mid-January, 1945) five million under the above described conditions. If so, the transfers agreed were a deliberate act of unbelievable cruelty. No genuinely Polish authority could even contemplate such an act.

It may, however, be surmised that the transfer agreements were only conceived as a propaganda measure. Then, after the lapse of the terms involved, we should be assured that, since Poles east of the Curzon Line had been allowed free choice of habitat, no Polish problem existed in Eastern Poland. Thus, over four million Poles would be left to gradual Sovietisation, a procedure much against their wishes. Again we may state that no genuinely Polish authority could endorse such a solution, equivalent to cutting off from the main body of the nation of one-sixth of it, especially in view of the tremendous losses sustained by the Poles during this war.

CHAPTER XXII

THE " PROVISIONAL GOVERNMENT "

The sixth winter of war in Europe was to be an eventful period for the people of Poland.

In mid-January, a mighty Red Army offensive started on their soil, and the slogan " On to Berlin " resounded powerfully, announcing the end of Nazi tyranny in Poland and arousing new hope.

Owing to the exemplary secrecy with which all Soviet military moves are enshrouded, the Lublin Committee men could not have foreseen when the new Red Army sweep to the West would start, and how far it would carry.

Nevertheless, they somehow adapted themselves to the new circumstances that military events were to bring about. As if by a wave of a magician's wand, the Committee disappeared, and a '' Polish Provisional Government '' arose.

Let us examine this '' Government.''

On December 31st, 1944, the National Council of the Homeland, suddenly increased to 105 '' deputies '' *unanimously* passed a '' law '' calling into being, in place of the Committee of National Liberation set up by the '' law '' of 22nd July, 1944, a '' Provisional Government of Poland.'' At the same time, the Chairman of the Council who was to appoint the new Government was assigned the title of President of the Council *by acclamation*. We may note in passing that the degree of unanimity as previously shown in all sittings both of the Council and the Committee was not very reminiscent of the ways of Western democracy.

On December 31st, Mr. Bierut, the Komintern agent, duly appointed the new Government. Its composition is as follows :

Premier and Minister for Foreign Affairs—Mr. Osubka-Morawski.

First Deputy-Minister—Władysław Gomółka.

Second Deputy-Premier—Stanisław Janusz.

Minister of National Defence—General Rola-Zymierski.

    ,, ,, Public Administration—Józef Maślanka.

    ,, ,, Public Security—Stanisław Radkiewicz.

    ,, ,, Finance—Konstanty Dąbrowski.

    ,, ,, Public Education—Stanisław Skrzeszewski.

    ,, ,, Labour, Public Welfare and Health—Wiktor Trojanowski.

    ,, ,, Agriculture and Agrarian Reforms—Edward Bertold.

    ,, ,, Communication—Jan Rabanowski.

   „ „ Industry—Hilary Minc.

   „ „ Supplies and Commerce—Teodor Piotrowski.

   „ „ Posts, Telegraphs and Telephones—Tadeusz Kapeliński.

   „ „ Justice—Edmund Zaleski.

   „ „ Information and Propaganda—Stefan Matuszewski.

Broadcasting from Lublin for the *News Chronicle* on December 31st, 1944, Stefan Litauer, an ex-official of the Polish Government, alleged that the " Provisional Government included five Socialists and five Peasants, four members of the " Polish Workers' Party," two members of the Democratic Party and one non-party member, General Zymierski. In the same broadcast—and this was the first admission of this to emanate from the official Lublin Station, Litauer termed the ' Polish Workers' Party ' as " Communist-equivalent." The following were described as " Socialists " : Morawski, Dąbrowski, Trojanowski, Matuszewski, Skrzeszewski presumably being the fifth. The " Peasants " were : Janusz, Maślanka, Bertold, Zaleski, the fifth being left unnamed. The Communists—for we prefer the straightforward term— were : Gomółka, Radkiewicz, Minc (the latter being described as such in a broadcast of the same day destined for the N.Y.T. in New York and London) with two others unrevealed. One of the " Democrats " may be named on the strength of the information previously quoted : Rzymowski.

Unfortunately we have some grounds for doubting the accuracy of this information. In actual fact the number of Communists in disguise among the members of the " Provisional Government " is far greater.

We may be excused for quoting at some length a statement by the Polish Socialist Party's Committee Abroad, published in the *Polish Daily* of January 9th, 1945 :

    " Among those composing the alleged central authority of the Polish Socialist Party in Lublin, the names of Messrs. Bolesław Drobner, alleged chairman of the

Supreme Council of the Polish Socialist Party, Edward Osubka-Morawski, alleged chairman of the Central Executive Committee of the Polish Socialist Party and Stefan Matuszewski, alleged secretary of the Central Executive Committee of the Polish Socialist Party, are known to us. We wish to state categorically that the above-mentioned never had and have not any right to make use of these titles. At the time of the outbreak of war, none of them sat either on the Central Executive Committee or on the Supreme Council of the Polish Socialist Party during the period, 1939-1944.

The statement continued :

'' Edward Osubka-Morawski left the Polish Socialist Party during the war and became a member of a newly-arisen group bearing the name of the Polish Socialist Workers' Party, the remains of which, after a number of breaches, took on the character of an accessory to the Polish Workers' Party (P.P.R.) the new name of the Communist Party of Poland. The former priest, Stefan Matuszewski, as far as we know, was never a member of the Polish Socialist Party.''

Further on, the statement continued :

'' All the above-mentioned alleged representatives of the Polish Socialist Party are usurpers, not empowered by the Polish working classes organised in the Polish Socialist Party to speak in their name. The reference made by the so-called ' provisional government ' in Lublin to the support given to it by the Polish Socialist Party and to that Party's participation in that government are thus a deception and abuse which we brand as such, and of which we warn the workers' Socialist movements all over the world.''

We think that the information contained in this statement allows us to state that Morawski and Matuszewski are just two Communists posing as Socialists. Of Skrzeszewski and General Zymierski, it has already been said that they were Communists.

Dąbrowski and Trojanowski are two names as yet unknown to anyone. Would it be safe to assume that they, too, might be Communists in Socialist disguise ?

For the time being we have to omit any discussion of the question whether the remainder of the " provisional government " members have or have not secretly joined the " Polish Workers' Party " and not only its ramifications as described above.

It seems entirely sufficient for our purpose to state that alongside the five acknowledged Communists, there are *at least* four other disguised Communists and that in a cabinet of 13 members these nine constitute an absolute majority likely to carry through any measure. They are indeed the core of the " provisional government."

Never before has any Polish government had a Communist majority. More than that, not a single Polish government of the 1918-1945 period has ever had any Communists in the Cabinet. The reason for this is that, as in this country—the Communists have always been a negligible minority.

Here, in the " provisional government " the Communists have suddenly become the core. This suggests something alien, something foreign : could it be Article 126 of the Soviet Constitution, according to which " the Communist Party . . . is the leading core of all organisations of the working class, both social and State " ?

PART IV

CHAPTER XXIII

POLICE RULE

Strict control of public administration, of the police, and of all propaganda means such as press and wireless are indispensable features of a totalitarian regime. In its bid for complete control of state machinery and the population, such a regime must also obtain a firm hold on the national armed forces so as to be sure of their unquestioning support should the regime be threatened either from within or from outside.

This method of seizing power was used by the Nazis in Germany. Their subjection of Western and Central Poland was on similar lines. However, the similarity did not extend very far.

In subjecting Poland, the Nazis first destroyed the Polish armed forces. Then they suppressed the entire Polish press, and, contrary to the Hague Convention of 1906, liquidated the Polish administrative, educational and judiciary systems. Only the remnants of autonomous local administration, of the ordinary police, led a precarious existence in the shadow of an enforced Nazi system manned by the Germans themselves and protected by the Gestapo, the S.S. and the Reichswehr.

Nevertheless, the Poles did not give up. Deprived of the possibility of open action, they went underground, and there recreated in the greatest secrecy part of the Polish pre-war administrative, educational and judiciary system which acted on the strength of the moral authority of the Polish national idea alone, recognised by the whole nation.

In this the Poles had only repeated in more perfect shape their own tradition dating from about eighty years previously, when, during a rising against the Russians a secret Polish administration was set up which worked effectively during the two years it lasted.

At first executive power was entrusted to a Government Delegate and 13 heads of departments. Later on, changes were effected formally acknowledging the great moral and actual authority of the heads of the Underground Administration by elevating the Delegate to the rank of Vice-Premier in the Polish Cabinet, while three of his heads of Departments were accepted into the Cabinet with the rank of Ministers. Legislative power was vested in a body first known as the Political Representation of the Homeland, and later renamed The Council of National Unity. All Polish parties such as the Socialists, the Peasants, the Christian Democrats, the National Democrats and the other smaller groups were represented on both the administrative and the legislative-political bodies.

A network of administrative regional authorities was formed in all voivodships and districts.

A Home Army Command was set up which controlled a whole military network composed of regimental or divisional units established on the pre-war model.

Deprived of their educational system, except for the primary schools which were allowed to carry on under Nazi supervision in the so-called Government-General, the Poles organised a whole network of secondary schools and even higher schools, which if imperfect and only fragmentary, tried hard to replace the educational facilities destroyed. Tens of thousands of Polish youth were thus able to learn in defiance of the Nazis, whose avowed aim it was to turn the Polish nation into a host of almost illiterate slaves working for the Reich. Diplomas given by the Underground Education Authority were usually confirmed by the Ministry of Education working in London.

Thus, despite constant persecution and the death of many who fell into the clutches of the Gestapo, a skeleton political, administrative, judiciary and educational system worked within certain limits, and was perhaps one of the most striking features in the Polish nation's struggle for freedom to live her own life.

When the Lublin Committee came to Poland, not only did it not protect the existing Underground system, but, despite the five years' resistance offered by that system to the Nazis, and the succour it had given to the Polish people, denounced it as " fascist," " collaborationist," and as working for the enemy. It is not difficult to find the reasons for these monstrous accusations. The Committee had decided to clear the field for its own system, and in this resolve it soon proved to be devoid of any scruples whatsoever. Thus, when, at the instruction of the Polish Government, the heads of districts, voivodships and military regions revealed themselves to the representatives of the Red Army, it was suggested to them as a rule that they should accede to the Committee. In the event of refusal to do so, which was only natural in view of their loyalty to the system for which they had worked for long weary years, they were arrested, put into detention camps or prisons, and deported to the East as " traitors."

Notwithstanding the real state of affairs, it was the accepted view of the Committee that the Polish territory constituted a political vacuum. Accordingly, a " Committee " administration was set up from above. Communal National Councils were imposed upon the boroughs. These delegated representatives to District National Councils. These, in turn, sent delegates to the Voivodship National Councils, upon which the superstructure of the National Council of the Homeland was erected. The latter had arrogated to itself the prerogatives of a Polish Parliament.

In order fully to understand the principles underlying this system, it must be borne in mind that it is an accurate copy of the system in existence in the Soviet Union. The Communal Council corresponds to the " Selsoviet," the District Council to the " Raysoviet " and the Voivodship Council to the " Oblsoviet." The only difference is the addition of the adjective " national."

It is essential to note that the system introduced by the Committee cannot be regarded as anything based on popular will. The representatives of the borough are usually enforced upon suddenly convoked meetings by a noisy minority, backed by Committee agents who do not spare threats if the meeting should prove stubborn and restive. The remainder of the structure does not rest even upon sham direct suffrage, but upon delegation to the higher Councils of those regarded as fully trustworthy and reliable by the agents of the Committee. This introduces the principle of indirect election, which has long been rejected in the Western Democracies as undemocratic.

The results of this system are already evident. All resolutions of the National Council of the Homeland, including that governing the formation of the " provisional government," and all other decrees relating to political, social and economic matters, have been adopted unanimously. There has not been even the slightest opposition.

The Committee has not yet bothered to adopt a law stating how the various councils should be elected. Even after half a year of rule it still adheres to the practice of calling meetings at which, after a series of fiery speeches by Communists, in their many disguises, Committee representatives propose a list of candidates which is usually unanimously accepted.

Two Ministries have been placed at the head of this administration : the Ministry of Public Administration and of Public Security. It is rather surprising that a Ministry of Public Security should have anything to do with the setting up of an allegedly popular administration ; nevertheless, this is so. A spokesman of this Ministry has admitted it himself in an interview given to the Committee's official daily paper, *Rzeczpospolita* : " First of all, we help all the national councils in rendering the administration more efficient. . . . We aim at creating such administrative organs as will ensure the individual, social and political interests of the nation." (Lublin broadcast of January 24th, 1945.) As a matter of fact, the two Ministries fulfil the same task, and for some time even formed one single body. Both act through the police, which, as in the Soviet Union, is composed of two services.

The first service is called " The People's Militia " (equivalent to the Workers' and Peasants' Militia of the U.S.S.R.), and it is their task to ensure order, to keep the registers and to protect the population against minor offenders. The second police service bears the name of " Special Security Service " (the Soviet equivalent being the N.K.V.D.). The importance of this service cannot be overestimated. It controls the political life of the country, and gives the final opinion as to the political reliability of the citizen. It is made up of elements wholly and blindly devoted to the regime, and well rewarded for their services (the pay being double that received by the " Militia ").

At present, the main duty of the Security Police is that of tracking down soldiers of the Home Army and the personnel of the Underground Administration. Special travelling units have been set up for this purpose to operate in forests and in mountainous regions which at the time of the Nazi occupation were the favourite hiding places of the larger reserves of the Home Army.

The system which we have endeavoured to describe here is now in its first stage of organisation, the more so as it began to take over territories recently freed from the Germans only in the latter half of January of this year. Many of the less important posts in the two Ministries and in the two police services have not yet been filled. Gaps are being filled mostly with specially trained foreign officials and officers imported from Russia, whilst new candidates are being prepared in special political police schools, the biggest of which has been set up at Biała Podlaska.

When the structure of the new administration is complete, it will undoubtedly provide a firm backbone for the new regime, and, whatever the opposition, will make a determined effort to seize the political leadership of the nation, crushing ruthlessly any attempt at criticism or free expression of public opinion.

CHAPTER XXIV

ENSLAVEMENT OF MIND

Another powerful tool of the totalitarian regime is the Press. Whilst the State administration's task is physically to enslave the citizens, the Press and propaganda organs related to it, such as radio and literary production, have to paralyse his mind and mould it according to the wishes of the rulers.

First of all, the reader is to be strictly separated from the world so that no ideas and no information could reach him which would tend to develop a critical attitude towards the regime. Secondly, all internal opposition is to be silenced. Third, all those writing for the Press or broadcasting on the wireless, are to be subordinated to one single propaganda centre, that of the Government.

In France, Britain, and the U.S.A., if the governments feel it necessary to introduce some measure of press control in war-time, a censorship is set up whose instructions or advice may be resented, but, usually, are freely challenged and criticised. In the totalitarian countries no such measure is necessary since all the press, all the broadcasting stations, all the printing presses and paper factories belong to the State. Therefore, no direct control is needed, and a perfect black-out is imposed on news and ideas. No one can make a speech, publish an article, or a pamphlet without previous consent by the authorities.

Immediately after the Committee's appearance at Chełm, an official daily organ was started under the name of *Rzecz-pospolita*. The name was strangely reminiseent of that of the official organ of the Polish Underground Movement,

Rzeczpospolita Polska. Later on, the names of popular organs of the various Polish parties were appropriated unscrupulously, such as *The Worker* ('' Robotnik '') of the Polish Socialist Party and *The Green Flag* (''Zielony Sztandar''), the organ of the Peasant Party. Both these papers have noble traditions of their own, and, in the autumn of 1939, when Polish political leaders established themselves in France, an old Socialist leader, the late Liberman, had restarted *The Worker* in Paris, whilst *The Green Flag* made its appearance at a later date in London, as the organ of the Peasant Party.

Further, the Committee restarted the Peasant Youth's pre-war weekly paper, *Wici*. The Committee's '' Democratic Party '' published a weekly under a pre-war title *The New Epoch* ('' Nowa Epoka ''). This organ was edited before the war by a group of democratic intelligentsia.

The idea of imitation coupled with appropriation of titles has been carried through consistently even with regard to the non-political press. The Committee's children's paper has been named *The Little Flame* ('' Płomyk ''), the reason being that in pre-war Poland, the Association of Teachers published a popular children's paper under that name.

Mr. Zymierski publishes military organs. He has not refrained from using the name of the pre-war Army daily *Poland in Arms* ('' Polska Zbrojna ''), which before the September catastrophe was in the hands of military men who could not be suspected of any Communist leanings. Now the paper is engaged in slandering the Home Army and the leaders of the Polish Army fighting in Holland and Italy. Nor has the monthly *Bellona*, a valuable professional military publication, been forgotten by the Committee, though the organ has appeared for several years in London. Lublin has already announced that it would soon be restarted.

Despite the variety of titles and the trends to represent, all these Committee papers are very much alike. The leading articles, political comment, and anything of any importance, appear as a rule in all the papers practically simultaneously both in openly Communist papers such as *The People's Voice* ('' Głos Ludowy '') and in papers alleged to represent the Socialists, the Peasants and the Democrats. The same information is repeated in all, the same slogans are used, and the same hysterical enthusiasm is displayed when publishing the lengthy speeches by Osubka-Morawski, Bierut or Zymierski. And that is hardly surprising for everything comes from one journalistic kitchen at the head of which we find a well-merited Stalinite Communist, Mr. Borejsza (Goldman) of whose role in the 1940 purge of brother-writers we have already spoken in a previous chapter.

Broadcasting in Poland was entrusted before the war to Radio Polskie Ltd.—equivalent to the B.B.C. Following the general line, the Committee called into being an organisation of its own under the pre-war name. A Communist whom we already mentioned, Mr. Billig, became its head, and the former Komintern Kościuszko station, which also had been under Mr. Billig's management, was closed down.

Although the '' Radio Polskie '' had announced that the radio network would be considerably expanded, an order was issued instructing the Poles to give up any radio sets they might have preserved, and hand them over to the authorities.

This order was posted in cities, towns, and villages, immediately after the Nazis were expelled, and it directed the Poles also to hand over to the authorities any weapons, that they might have possessed. It also enforced registration of typewriters, gestetners and printing presses.

The meaning of the order is clear. The Lublin Station must have grasped its grotesque character—weapons being put on the same level as radio sets—and it hastened to give a queer explanation : alleging that '' the use of unauthorised radio sets might interfere with the wireless system '' and that '' unauthorised equipment would be confiscated and users punished.'' (broadcast on January 1st, 1945).

We should be greatly surprised, if, some day, the **B.B.C.** should decide that private wireless sets hindered its useful work, and enforced an administrative decree by virtue of which the police would be authorised to take away all the sets from the people.

However, the Lublin radio has given the assurance that the listeners would receive licences. We shall not be far wrong if we surmise that, as in other totalitarian countries, licences will be issued only to those few who enjoy special confidence in police quarters. In any case, the simple citizen will, at best, have to content himself with a set limited to local wireless stations, in practice, however, official loudspeakers will do. The loudspeakers will be placed everywhere, in the streets, in factories, restaurants, and railway stations, and will undoubtedly be presented as visible proof of how the democratic Committee cares for the popularity of the wireless.

Drab unanimity will pour over the citizen through all the means at the disposal of the Committee and its " parties," through which, as we rightly fear, drop by drop, the cult of a totalitarian system and hatred towards anything else not conforming to it, will be instilled, until the citizen, worn out by years of brutal discipline and misery, becomes malleable and apathetic clay in the hands of the " Polish Workers' Party."

CHAPTER XXV

THE FOUR COMMITTEE PARTIES

Freedom of political opinion is the elementary basis of democracy. Every citizen is entitled to profess such political views as seem right to him. Those of similar views form associations whose aim it is to convince the rest of the community of the rightness of their outlook and of the necessity of putting them into practice. Thus, the system of free political parties arises which, in turn, constitutes the basis of a parliamentary system. Based upon an entirely different political philosophy, totalitarian States do not recognise any groups opposed to their policy. The Governments of Nazi Germany, Fascist Italy and Soviet Russia are based on one single party conceived as one of the most important constituents of the State itself.

The Lublin Committee has adopted an intermediate system. As stated above, it disposes of a shadow party system created by the Communist Party, itself concealed behind the mask of the " Polish Workers' Party." For this purpose the names of old and popular Polish parties have been used, thus giving the newly created system an appearance of reality.

In order to understand this invention which is not lacking in originality, a few remarks are necessary concerning pre-war political life in Poland.

As already stated, the leaders of the Communist Party in Poland were only too conscious of the unpopularity of their doctrine among the Polish masses. However, the adoption of a new name was in itself not enough. They knew that Poland had old political traditions of her own and that the Poles are attached to their parties which existed even before 1914 in all the three parts into which Poland was divided : in Russian, Prussian and Austrian Poland. These parties had greatly contributed to the re-establishment and maintenance of independence.

Therefore, within the framework of the general artificial system of power set up on Polish soil, unscrupulous use was made of the names of the established parties so as to be able to boast of having the support of all the Polish political trends.

In spite of this, the Communist plot of falsification forgot three political parties which existed before the war. These were : the National Democratic Party, the Jewish Zionist Party and the Christian Democratic Party, the latter better known in Poland under its new name of Labour Party.

The National Democratic Party amongst whose founders were such men as Roman Dmowski, one of the foremost

Polish promoters of complete reconciliation with Russia, Tsarist and Soviet, has for forty years represented the views of the Polish Right Wing, and was one of the strongest parties in several Polish parliaments. One may or may not share its views, but it would be difficult to imagine that this powerful body of Polish political opinion should have altogether disappeared from the stage. Similarly no Left Wing magician could destroy the British Tories by mere incantation, whatever were the charges he might level against their policy.

The Christian Democrat Party, with less following, represented the views of moderate social reformers as expressed in the famous Papal encyclical De Rerum Novarum. However, in the setting up of the Lublin shadow system, this Party was not included.

The greatest possible use has been made of the labels of the two other parties, the Polish Socialist Parties and the Peasant Party.

These are representative parties of the Left Wing with respectable and noble traditions. Their members have taken part in the Polish Government and in its underground branch, the Political Representation of the Homeland, later re-named " Council of National Unity." There is no leader of any standing who would have agreed to co-operate with the Communist Committee. Were the Committee to succeed in attracting part of the former followers of the two parties, which is most unlikely, mere decency would demand that a new name be found, as is the practice in all civilised countries. This the Communists would not do. They are far more interested in acquiring a false façade, than in getting real support. Therefore, after a period during which halfway names were used such as Peasant Party Opposition Group and Polish Workers' Socialist Party, no scruples were shown in appropriating the names of the two parties in their literal form.

The head of the two " parties " were men about whom neither the Polish people nor the party men better acquainted with all personalia of Polish pre-war politics had ever heard much before. Mr. Osubka-Morawski, the Chairman of the Lublin Committee and a member of the Communist Party found himself elevated to the rank of Chairman of the " Polish Socialist Party." Before the war he was secretary of the Polish Socialist Youth Party organisation in a small town in Central Poland; later he became a clerk of a co-operative of flats in Warsaw. Such were the qualifications fitting him to represent the Party of which many leaders had been arrested by the Soviet authorities and deported to the U.S.S.R. during 1939-41 and since July, 1944, either to die in imprisonment, or never to be heard of again. The fact that M. Morawski changed his convictions during the war and acceded to the Polish Workers' Party is apparently of no consequence.

The post of deputy chairman was reserved for another man with a Socialist past oscillating between Communism and Socialism and, after many dissensions with the P.S.P., finally ejected therefrom in 1936. We do not know for certain whether M. Drobner has, or has not, joined the mother party of the " Polish Workers " but in his case, this seems completely irrelevant.

The newly created " Polish Socialist Party " cannot boast of the participation of any single member of the authoritative organs of the real Party, nor of any member of the Trade Unions organisations, or any Seym or Senate Deputies.

The chairmanship of the Peasant Party was entrusted to Andrzej Witos. This was another attempt at political falsification. As we have already stated, Andrzej Witos is a half-brother of the great Peasant leader, Wincenty, twice Prime Minister of Poland, whose name resounded vigorously throughout modern Polish history, and who, seriously ill, was kept in detention by the Nazis during almost the whole of the war. Thus, the idea of promoting Wincenty's brother was not bad. However, his sponsors underestimated the Polish peasant's political shrewdness. When it became clear that no one was taken in by the same surname, and that a sharp distinction was being made between the two brothers, Andrzej Witos was simply thrown into the political dustbin. As often happens under a totalitarian regime, someone else took his position as vice-chairman of the Committee and of the chairman of the '' Peasant Party,'' and Witos has not been heard of since. It would not be very surprising, though this might seem rather a rash supposition—that he was again deported to the Republic of Komi, whence he had been released by the Soviet authorities and asked to join the Patriots' Union.

A Mr. Janusz replaced him as Chairman of the '' Party,'' an obliging person, of whose services the pre-war colonels had availed themselves for the purpose of splitting the (real) Peasant Party, and who was only too glad to serve the new masters of Poland. Naturally enough, he is a member of the '' Polish Workers' Party.''

A '' Democratic Party '' was also included in this artificial system. It is true that a party of this name existed in pre-war Poland. It was a party with some following among the intelligentsia. Being a new party it did not have the time to make for itself a position among the traditional parties which already existed.

It is difficult to state what were the reasons behind the using of this party. The most reasonable would be supposition that it was the well sounding name suggestive of Democracy. Utterly unintelligible was, however, the fact that the chairmanship of the '' Party '' was entrusted to someone who found himself before the war ostracised by fellow writers on account of his unmasked plagiarism from Bertrand Russell. Apparently, the Communist Party could not find anyone with better antecedents.

The shadow party system created and worked by the Communists, is in actual fact a branch of the Communist mother party, and has one striking feature—that there is not one single matter, social or political, on which these parties could be found to disagree. Their unanimity is uncanny.

However perfect the organisation, strange slips can be detected from time to time which are either due to parts not having been learnt by heart or may be ascribed to a nonchalant neglect of public opinion, which is apparently expected to swallow everything. Thus, M. Czechowski, a prominent Communist, has been presented to the public as a non-party Nationalist and as a representative of the Peasant Party. A certain Monsieur Grubecki, a former student of Lvov University, then in the ranks of the Jew haters, has been "elected" to secretaryship of the "Peasant Party."

Many such slips have occurred, which must have strained the credulity of the public opinion supposed to take the " Parties " at their face value.

In totalitarian States the Master Party is part of the Government itself. As such it is its obligation to fulfil certain national tasks which under the democratic system are reserved for the executive organs of the State. In Soviet Russia the Communist Party is charged with carrying out propaganda campaigns in favour of repairing tractors, increasing the amount of corn to be sown, etc. The Lublin " parties " also undertake such tasks. As stated many times on the Lublin wireless the " parties " have taken part in carrying out the call-up for the army and in dividing up the land. Thus, the four Lublin " parties " are organs of the Government equally with the Master Party of the totalitarian State ; the only difference being that the single party has been split in Lublin into four allegedly independent ramifications.

The Division into four " parties " has its practical aim. Its mission is to create the illusion that a democratic system has been set up in the Committee's Poland and that the Committee really represents the nation.

A special task is reserved for this sham system during the future elections for the Polish parliament, which the Committee wants to carry out as soon as the enemy is cleared out of Poland. This is to be done during the presence of the

Red Army on Polish soil and before any of the Polish detainees in Russia and elsewhere are given an opportunity to return and while all truly representative bodies of the Polish Nation are either crushed or deprived of any possibility of taking their share in public life.

*   *   *

As it seems, the new organisation of the community introduced by the Committee will be of still greater consequence. Each section of the community is to have only one organisation and no other organisations are allowed. The peasants have been presented with a "Peasant Self-Help" where all the key posts have been taken by the "Polish Workers' Party." As the "Self-Help" is the only organisation allowed and as it has received certain essential privileges such as assignments of grain or agricultural implements for distribution, it is impossible to hold aloof from it.

The trade unions have been formed along the same lines. By the end of a few weeks each section of labour had been organised into its own trade union. Henceforth, no other union would exist, let alone act. In this way, by a stroke of the pen, the workers have been subjected to the leadership of one single political party. We need not stress that this amounts to denying labour's fundamental right to organise itself on a voluntary basis with adequate safeguards for the freedom of political opinion. The Fascist trade unions conception quite unexpectedly found its realisation on Polish soil at a time when the memory of their creator had been successfully obliterated in liberated Italy.

At the end of December, 1945, the Congress of the "Peasant Party" adopted a resolution by virtue of which all those Peasant leaders at present abroad who would not accede to the new "Peasant Party," would be deprived of Polish nationality. On the other hand, the "Polish Socialist Party" on February 27th, 1945, adopted a resolution to the effect that all those Socialist and trades unions leaders who took part in the Underground Movement during the Nazi occupation are struck off the lists of Party members. Thus, no measure to safeguard the future of the totalitarian system introduced by the Committee seems to have been neglected.

CHAPTER XXVI

PEASANTS AND WORKERS DECEIVED

The twisted intentions of the Soviet-sponsored Lublin Committee are best revealed as such in the set of economic and social reforms announced. and in part already carried out.

It is common knowledge that South-Eastern Europe has for long been in need of reform in almost every respect. Much progressive thought has been devoted to this problem, and many demands formulated in the South-East-European parliaments and press. The area is one of the most backward on the Continent. The countryside is overpopulated, and small farm holdings prevail incapable of satisfying the barest minimum of the owners' needs. Accordingly, the reformers demanded the development of industry into which the surplus population could be diverted, and the division of large land estates so that the dwarf peasant holdings might be adequately enlarged.

In the period 1918-20 the problem of agrarian reform had become *the* most acute problem in the countries of South-Eastern Europe, especially in those which had regained independence as a result of the first world war. The parcellation of large estates aroused much passion and was much easier than costly industrial development, hardly possible without financial help from abroad.

In Poland, Parliament adopted in 1920 a law of agrarian reform providing for the gradual parcellation of large estates and the sale of land thus acquired to peasants on conditions of long-term credit.

Before the present war broke out, about one-third of the land liable had been parcelled, 2,655,000 out of about $7\frac{1}{2}$ million hectares of arable land. The representatives of the Peasant Party and of the Socialist Party constantly criticised the Government for alleged delay in carrying out the reform and demanded that the remainder of the land should be parcelled out as quickly as possible. The then Minister of Agriculture, Mr. Poniatowski, was also attacked for creating holdings of nine hectares which were rightly condemned as insufficient for the upkeep of a peasant family. At the same time, the parties of the Polish Left-Wing were realising that even the parcellation of the remainder of the land liable to the agrarian reform could not satisfy the Polish peasantry since there was too little land altogether. Therefore, the problem of industrialisation and of an improvement of the methods of farming took an ever more prominent place in the programme of both the Left-Wing parties.

The programme of the Communist Party, both in Poland and in the other countries of South-Eastern Europe, was entirely different. Faithful to the principles of orthodox Marxism, they aimed at introducing collective economy also in agriculture. However, they knew only too well that collectivisation would arouse widespread resentment amongst the peasants who were used and attached to individual farming, and that, should any attempt be made to enforce collectivist measures, a popular mutiny would break out, which would be dangerous for the unwelcome reformers. The year 1939 enriched the Communists' experience in that respect, when the peasants of Eastern Poland had to be deported *en masse* to Siberia for refusal to comply with collectivisation. Therefore, the " Polish Workers' Party " decided to announce a land reform which though not in accordance with their real programme, was likely—as they thought—to prove a political success. An order was issued on September 6th, 1944, which provided for the parcellation of all holdings above 50 hectares, to be completed by December 20th. 1944, i.e., within three months and 20 days. The time allowed suggested Stakhanovist tempo. The quality of work did not matter. Anyone with any knowledge of agricultural problems knows that a reform of that extent requires thousands of specialists to measure up and to divide the land, to assess the value of soil, and to distribute it among the peasantry. Therefore, we may safely surmise that the real objective was a short-lived propaganda success.

The opportunity was eagerly seized upon for circulating once more the legend about Poland's reactionary landlords, hostile to the reform, as so many other legends and stories for ignorants. It would be superfluous to engage here in wider polemics, let us however state that in 1938 the big landed estates constituted in Poland only 12 per cent of agricultural land, whereas in this country the percentage is somewhat higher.

As it was to be expected, the Committee indulged in an orgy of self-laudation meant to create the impression that it was able to carry out a reform of which the '' reactionary '' Poland proved incapable.

The Committee has at best only speeded up the carrying out of the old law of agrarian reform from which whole paragraphs have been copied without any alteration, and this has been done in a way harmful to the interests of the peasants. The Committee territory comprised up to mid-January, 1945, not counting the front belt, not more than 400 thousands hectares of reformable land, and about 440 thousand dwarf peasant holdings. Thus, one holding averaged about 0.9 ha. Adding 110 thousands of landless peasantry to the number of 440 thousand landed peasants we should obtain the number of 550 thousand candidates to getting land under the reform which was equivalent to one peasant entitled to receive 0.7 hect. Even the greatest reformer's zeal would not multiply the quota of available land. Parcellation could not satisfy the hunger for land of the landless. The speed with which the '' reform '' has been carried out with the help of the armed forces, the N.K.V.D., and the agitators of the Committee '' parties '' could have brought nothing but harm. It may be sufficient to point out that the newly created farm holdings have received no livestock, no credits and no agricultural equipment of any kind whatsoever.

Hidden deep behind the Committee land reform is the idea of collectivisation, the real aim of the Communist manœuvre. In virtue of the reform law issued by the Committee men, the new holdings could be increased only up to 5 hectares. Let us remember that before the war, the Polish Government was criticised for setting up holdings of 9 hectares, which were thought by the champions of the peasants to be too small to ensure the livelihood of a family.

Lublin reduced the quota to 5 hectares, thus showing utter disregard for the political shrewdness of the Polish peasant. The latter at once understood that the Lublin reformers aim at creating the smallest possible farm holdings, unworkable, so as to be able to carry out more easily collectivisation in the future. He remembered that in 1918 the Russian Communists came to power with the slogan '' land and peace,'' and that parcellation was soon followed by collectivisation of the parcelled land.

This time the Lenin manœuvre did not succeed. In October, 1944, disturbances took place amongst the peasantry, and the carrying out of the reform was suspended. The Committee found a scapegoat in the person of its own Vice-Chairman and head of the Department of Agriculture, Mr. A. Witos. Army and police units were called out to quell the disturbances, whilst the Committee announced that the landlords and the agents of the '' reactionary '' Polish Government were at the root of the trouble. They had allegedly been sabotaging the salutary reform. Afterwards, it was announced that the reform had been carried out, and, for the benefit of the peasant masses, restive and disappointed, an announcement was made that all those who had not received any land under the reform, would be given land conquered from the Germans in East Prussia, German Pomerania, and the region of the Oder.

We have dwelt at some length on the problem of agrarian reform as carried out by the Lublin Committee, since, as we feel, it is a problem more complicated and requiring explanation if it is to be understood in its true perspectives in the West-European countries.

The solution arrived at by the Committee is only likely to cause new difficulties in future. It is obvious that it has been dictated by propaganda needs, and not by the interests of the peasant, which is fully understandable if we take into account the fact that the reform has come from the East and that it has been inspired by people with no ties whatsoever with rural Poland.

The social and economic programme of the Committee does not need any such detailed examination. It has been rather clearly outlined in a speech by Mr. Osubka-Morawski delivered in January 2nd, 1945, the day when he was appointed head of the " Provisional " Government.

Contrary to the July Manifesto of the Committee, Osubka's speech completely ignores the question of civic liberties, which thus seems to have ceased to exist even officially. On the contrary, it enumerates penalties to be imposed on the population for all sorts of " offences " which will be dealt with in detail later on, and it even introduces such totalitarian practices as compulsory labour and deportation of the non-working population from towns. The question may be asked where that population is to be deported, as it is hardly to be expected that they could be transferred to the notoriously overpopulated *Polish* countryside. It may also be asked whether the " non-working " population means those who do not want to work or simply victims of unemployment, which may easily arise in the economic chaos produced by Lublin. In any case such a practice would constitute a menace not only to the civic, but the elementary human rights of Polish citizens.

In the only case where he mentions any freedom at all, namely, the freedom of instruction, Osubka hastens to add : " We are resolved to sweep away all existing anti-democratic tendencies in schools." With even a vague knowledge of the Lublin language the interpretation does not present any difficulties.

Religious matters or freedom of religious worship are not mentioned in Osubka's speech.

Contrary to the July Manifesto which promised the abolition or limitation of requisitions and quotas, Osubka now announces a most rigorous extraction of contributions, stating that " all the political authorities and economic organisations must realise that procrastination connected with supplies will not only not be tolerated but severely punished." A special Ministry of Supplies has been set up to extract the quotas from the peasants. In actual fact, the Red Army is imposing not only quotas, but also contributions. In a number of known cases and contrary to the previous " agreements " which stipulated for a fixed, though very high quota of grain, etc., the Soviet military authorities confiscated the entire crops. As a rule, the quotas are 20 per cent. higher than those levied by the Germans.

Passages in Osubka's speech dealing with the position of the Polish workers under the Lublin system are of particular interest. Twice in his speech Osubka demands of an " enlightened " Polish worker a maximum war effort and a tightening of discipline. What this may mean is shown by the recent militarisation of the Polish railways and the subordination of Polish railwaymen to the military penal code. It need hardly be emphasised that a popular and democratic Polish Government would never have needed to subject civilian workers to military discipline.

As far as wages are concerned, Osubka says : " To increase the output of labour there shall be introduced a system of bonuses for firms and for individual manual and non-manual workers, to be paid in cash and in food and clothing.

Without going into a detailed analysis of the statement and the system of wages it promises, it may be taken for granted that in any case this means a thorough exploitation of Polish labour.

Worst of all, Polish workers are being threatened by forced labour and deportations from towns to undefined destination. . . . " We shall not hesitate to introduce compulsory labour and to evacuate the non-working population from larger towns,'' says the Lublin " Premier.'' Forced labour has been imposed on millions of Europeans by Hitlerite Germany and it always seemed to be one of the shameful evils we were fighting against. The same totalitarian measure is now being reintroduced by the " democratic '' Lublin administration.

Chapter XXVII

RESISTANCE GROUPS STAMPED OUT

A minority government cannot assert itself otherwise than by means of coercion. Regrettable as it is, this truth has found ample illustration in the rule established on Polish territory by the Committee and its sponsors.

We are in the sixth year of the war. Since the autumn of 1939, the Polish nation has suffered bloody Nazi oppression, the worst ever experienced in that part of Europe. In addition, this nation has ungrudgingly been giving the blood of her best sons for her own and other peoples' freedom.

Liberty has dawned for Paris, Brussels, even for Rome, the ex-Fascist Rome, after much less suffering and in spite of less single-minded policies. Not so for Poland.

The old tyranny, that of the Nazis, with its acts of unbelievable cruelty and its crazy passion for annihilation, was at least understandable in one point. The Nazi was frankly an enemy. He came to destroy and did not make any pretence of friendship. He was unable to gain the collaboration of any section of the nation. The situation was clear and unequivocal.

Now there came someone with whom the Polish nation wanted to live on honourable and neighbourly terms. This hope, however, was only too quickly shattered.

A noisy handful of Polish Communists came in to provide cover for the policy of coercion. They were determined to crush any opposition, and this by all the means at their disposal.

Their main object was to crush the Polish Home Army.

This combat organisation was composed of Poles of all shades of political opinion, except for the none-too-numerous extremists. It ·had fought for five long years against the Nazis. Wherever the Red Army approached in its westward victorious drive, the well-trained and enthusiastic fighters of the Home Army were rising in masses, on the instruction of the Polish Government, to crown their five-year lonely struggle with yet one more feat of arms, this time in direct support of their Russian comrades.

Yet in Soviet and Polish-Communist eyes, the Home Army had one fault. It was not Communist-led, and, indeed, it certainly did not strive to establish a Poland organised on Soviet lines. Their idea of Poland was that of a country with a liberal democratic parliamentary regime with several parties contesting elections. In this they were in full agreement with some 98 per cent. of the nation.

The Committee could not have avowed this as the real reason for persecution. Something else had to be found, both for foreign and for internal consumption. Therefore, the Home Army was mendaciously branded as " not fighting against the Nazi enemy," and as " Fascist," or " reactionary." In some cases, allegations were put forward that its members had involved themselves in clashes with Communists, or even—supreme nonsense—with the Red Army.

Once their role as the vanguard of the Red Army's advance had ended, detachments of the Home Army were surrounded by the Russians, disarmed, the officers and part of the men arrested, the rest usually being forcibly enrolled into the Soviet-Polish Army of Generals Zymierski and Berling. This procedure has been the rule throughout Polish territory which, though the Red Army's share, naturally enough, had been the greater, had thus been jointly liberated from the Nazi yoke. We may instance this by giving several specific cases.

On July 25th, 1944, the disarmament was started of Home Army detachments forming the 27th Infantry Division, which immediately before the coming of the Russians had, after a costly struggle, liberated two towns in Central Poland, Kock and Lubartów and the surrounding districts. Kock, as the reader may remember, was the scene of the last battle between Polish regular forces and the Nazis in the autumn of 1939.

From July 22nd to July 24th, 1944, units of the Home Army took part in the fighting round Lublin, the future seat of the Committee. As long as the battle went on, the attitude of the Russians was correct and loyal. However, as soon as the front had moved farther westwards, it underwent a fundamental change. The Moor had done his job. The nearby death-camp of Majdanek where the Nazis had murdered hundreds of thousands of people, mostly Poles, was soon filled with new prisoners, Home Army officers and soldiers, with a sprinkling of members of the Civilian Underground Administration. This was supreme irony. True, the Majdanek stoves no longer worked, the chimneys of the death-factory no longer exhaled their sickening smoke. Nevertheless, a prison is a prison, and forcible deportation to far-away places in the U.S.S.R. was at least partial decease, even if there might have been the hope of some future return to Poland.

As early as the beginning of August, 1944, news had come to this country of new detention camps set up for the Home Army and for the civilian resistance men.

In the latter half of August, 1944, information was already forthcoming about a camp in the distant Ukraine, at Kharkov. Here, besides the Home Army men, came many soldiers and officers who, after having been forcibly enrolled in the Soviet-Polish Army in the U.S.S.R. had not been cautious enough to suppress what they felt.

Around Dębica and Krosno, in Southern Poland, co-operation between the Home Army and the Red Army had been of the smoothest during the month of August, 1944. A lively exchange of information concerning the strength and the position of the common Nazi enemy had been going on. All German soldiers captured by Home Army detachments were delivered to Red Army prisoner-of-war camps. In some encounters, the two armies had fought not only shoulder-to-shoulder, but also under joint local command. However, this did not prevent disarmament and arrests when the Moor had done his job.

When in mid-August, 1944, the commander of the Warsaw rising issued an S.O.S. call to Home Army units to come to the assistance of the Capital, the detachments operating in the Siedlce area subordinated themselves operationally to the Soviet Command and asked for permission to march. Permission was readily granted, and thereupon the Home Army units joined the Soviet forces. It was then that the unexpected happened. The Soviet Command ordered the disarmament of these units. This instance is one of many, and it is thus clear that if any help did succeed in reaching Warsaw, it was only due to the few Home Army units which, at great cost to themselves, broke through Nazi lines in the part of Poland then still under German occupation.

By the end of September, 1944, it was estimated that over 21,000 Home Army men had been arrested. Only those men and officers of the Home Army were set free who, after a period of imprisonment in abominable conditions, had agreed to sign a declaration to the effect that they were ready to serve under General Zymierski. It was a painful and humiliating step to have to take, and they were not spared further humiliation, as they were then assigned to special penal units of the Soviet-Polish Army.

All the time, it should be remembered, frantic propaganda was being carried on by the Committee press and radio as well as at meetings, at which Communist agitators, to the great indignation of the population, who know better, denounced the Home Army men as " bandits," " fascists," " murderers," " reactionaries " and " traitors."

A whole set of detention camps was set up around Siedlce, with the Krześlin camp as the main one, in which the arrested members of the Home Army and of the civilian Underground Administration were kept *en masse*. On November 13th, 1944, 2,500 detainees were thence taken away to the U.S.S.R. and further systematic deportation was started.

The partial failure of mobilisation for the Zymierski-Berling Army, due chiefly to the twisted policies of the Committee, was blamed upon the Home Army and the Polish Underground. This was sheer nonsense, because even if the Home Army had not existed, and at that time it had already been almost completely crushed by the repressive measures applied, the mobilisation was bound to fail. Even though starved of adequate information during the period of Nazi rule, and one-sidedly poisoned by Committee propaganda, the Polish people had quickly understood what sort of Poland was being prepared for them. However, there was still the liquidation of the Home Army west of the Vistula in store, and therefore propaganda had to be kept up. No wonder, then, that the Committee's chairman, Mr. Osubka-Morawski, declared on September 11th, 1944 :

> "We have to condemn uncompromisingly the anti-State and criminal appeals of the London reactionaries to boycot the mobilisation, doing it as they do out of motives of base political gambling . . . The Nation will not deny us the right to apply against traitors and anti-State elements" the punishment prescribed by the "law." (Moscow broadcast by the Union of Polish Patriots).

In a Manifesto to the regions recently liberated from the Nazi yoke, the National Council of the Homeland and the " provisional government " announced that they " would not hesitate to use the sharpest possible measures to render harmless the enemies of the nation.'' (A Moscow broadcast of January 20th, 1945.)

During January, 1945, the Lublin Committee Station allowed several foreign correspondents to reveal some of the terrorist measures applied against the Home Army and the civilian Underground. William Lawrance, broadcasting for the " New York Times '' stated on January 9th that " a certain number of arrests were still necessary to combat anti-Government activity,'' and " there was no effort to keep this a secret.'' On January 7th, Georges Champennois, French News Agency correspondent, admitted that the Lublin " government '' " had already arrested important leaders of the anti-national opposition and officers of its military organisation, the so-called Home Army.''

Foreign support alone had rendered it possible for the Committee thus to rule with the iron hand of terror. It is regrettable that this foreign support should have been lent at all, because terror is never the means for achieving honourable and neighbourly collaboration amongst nations, and it will not be easy to dispel the bitter memories it will have left in the minds of the Polish people.

SUMMING UP

We herewith conclude our study.

We have presented to the reader the doings of a handful of Communists who, acting with ruthless resolution according to a prearranged plan, have seized power in Poland against the will of the overwhelming majority of the Polish nation. We have shown how a " Polish '' Army has been formed under the command of Soviet officers and how it has been moulded by experts in political education. We also have drawn the picture of a group of men, hitherto unknown to the nation, who proclaimed themselves a " National Council of the Homeland,'' subsequently becoming a '' Committee for National Liberation '' and then a self-styled '' Government.'' We have exposed the mechanism of fictitious political parties. We have witnessed the setting up of a totalitarian regime with the help of the secret police, insincere slogans and a forged press. We have told of how heroic Warsaw was left to die, and how the whole Polish Resistance Movement was subsequently denounced as '' traitors,'' '' Fascists,'' or '' reactionaries,'' only to be arrested and deported eastwards outside the territory claimed by the Committee as their '' Poland.'' We also have elucidated the true sense of the social reforms which the Committee men have bestowed upon the Polish people.

All these doings have been committed in the name of the people and Democracy, allegedly for the people of Poland. The names of national heroes have been dragged out of the arsenal of history and misapplied, the names and the tradition of the parties have been appropriated, even the titles of press organs, so as to mislead public opinion inside the country as well as abroad. History has not known yet a forgery on such a scale, nor can the peoples of the world remember a sham prepared with so much premeditation and forethought by a tiny minority supported by a foreign power and its secret police.

Since the Committee men have attended already to almost every sphere of national life, the only performance that still remains to be staged is elections to Parliament. A special technical bureau has already been set up attached to the '' Ministry '' of Public Security and styled a '' Citizens' Technical Committee,'' and it will be its task to take care of the elections. The four sham parties will join the contest, and the elector will not be allowed to vote for any candidates not acknowledged and put forward by one of the four Communist Party ramifications in disguise. The genuine leaders of the people will have been rendered '' harmless,'' if they do not succeed in time in escaping the clutches of the new Gestapo and taking refuge in democratic countries. The parliament that will thus be " elected " will approve of all the Committee's doings, and will express consent to half of Poland being handed over to the U.S.S.R.

Will it be the final act of the drama of the Polish nation ? We do not know. We cannot foretell how long it will be necessary to keep up the fiction of an allegedly independent and allegedly democratic Poland. When this fiction will have fulfilled its role, the question will have to be settled of how to organise the existence and life of those nations, Poland being one of them, whose culture, national consciousness and tradition diverge so widely from that of Russia's. The problem has already been outlined in a letter by Joseph Stalin written to Lenin on June 12th, 1920 and preserved in the archives of the Lenin Institute in Moscow :

" I received on June 11th your draft of points to be considered at the Second Congress of the Komintern in connection with the national and colonial problem. At the present moment, I am unable to give a detailed and exhaustive opinion on these (I have no time) but I can point out one deficiency.

" I have in mind the fact that no mention has been made there about confederation, as one of the transition forms of rapprochement between the workers of the various nations.

" For the nations constituting the old Russia, our (Soviet) type of federation can and must be regarded as of the greatest assistance on the road towards international unity. The reasons are obvious : these national groups either had no state organisation in the past or had long ago lost it, so that the Soviet (centralised) type of federation could be grafted on without any special friction.

" The same cannot be said of those national groups not included in the old Russia as independent formations but having developed a specific state organisation of their own, and which, if they become Soviet, will perforce have to enter into some State relation with Soviet Russia: Take for instance a future Soviet Germany, Poland,

Hungary or Finland. It is doubtful whether these nations, who have their own State, their own army, their own finances, would, after becoming Soviet, at once agree to enter into a federal relationship with Soviet Russia of the Bashkir or Ukrainian type (in your minutes you differentiate between the Bashkir and the Ukrainian federal relationship, but, in actual fact, there is no difference or so little that it amounts to nothing) : they would regard federation of the Soviet type as a form of reducing their national independence and as an attempt against it.

" I do not doubt that the most acceptable form of rapprochement to these nationalities would be confederation (a union of independent States). I am leaving out the backward nationalities, e.g., Persia, Turkey, in relation to whom or for whom the Soviet type of federation and federation in general would be still more unacceptable.

" Bearing all this in mind, I think that it is indispensable to include at some point in your minute on the transition forms of rapprochement between the workers of the various nations the mention of *confederation* (alongside federation). Such an amendment would lend your proposals more elasticity, enrich them with one more transition form of rapprochement as described and would render State rapprochement with the Soviet easier to the national groups which did not previously form part of old Russia."

However, it may be that forces will be roused amongst the nations of the world whose impact will prove equal to the task of averting the ruin of real democracy and genuine freedom of individual human beings and of nations. The hope may be cherished that, amongst many other similar problems, the problem of Poland, Britain's first ally in this war, will strengthen the conscience and reinvigorate the honour of the United Nations, to demand the fulfilment of the principles for which millions of men have given their lives.

If any practical suggestions are to be made here, it seems to us that we should urge upon the Soviet Union to withdraw her armies and, above all, her secret police and her officials, from Polish territory, and that all those Poles be restored to Poland who left their country during the war, first of all the soldiers, airmen, sailors, who have fought at the side of the United Nations, the deportees and detainees deprived of their freedom, and the common civilians.

Subsequently, conditions ought to be created by a common effort of the United Nations for the carrying out of genuinely free and democratic elections, in which all parties and all men and women could participate. Then, a Government should be elected without outside pressure and without threat of foreign bayonets from beyond the frontiers of Poland, into whose hands the legal Polish Government would hand over its powers. Such a Government would have the sincere allegiance of the people.

No one's prestige would suffer thereby. Quite the contrary.

It would seem that this is not much to ask. This is all that Britain's faithful ally, Poland, asks for.